ASPEN PUBLISHERS

Instructor's Manual and Test Bank

to accompany

WILLS, TRUSTS, AND ESTATES
Essential Tools for the New York Paralegal

Second Edition

Ilene S. Cooper

Test Bank and Answers to Questions prepared by
Ann H. Still
Finger Lakes Community College

 Wolters Kluwer
Law & Business

AUSTIN   BOSTON   CHICAGO   NEW YORK   THE NETHERLANDS

To contact Customer Care, e-mail customer.care@aspenpublishers.com,
call 1-800-234-1660, fax 1-800-901-9075, or mail correspondence to:

Aspen Publishers
Attn: Order Department
PO Box 990
Frederick, MD 21705

Printed in the United States of America.

1 2 3 4 5 6 7 8 9 0

ISBN 978-0-7355-6380-3

TABLE OF CONTENTS

INTRODUCTION

The relationship between student and teacher is best fulfilled when both parties share a commitment to appreciating and understanding the subject matter and its practical application. From the instructor's perspective, this necessarily requires a considered analysis of case law, as well as current developments in the field. Towards this end, this instructor's manual should serve to enhance classroom instruction by providing the full text of the principal cases cited in the course book, as well as a discussion of their use as precedent. Additionally, the manual highlights areas of significance referred to in the course book which are deserving of additional comment and explanation. This should aid the students in their comprehension of the material as well as provide a basis for thought-provoking questions for students to consider.

In furtherance of the practical aspects of the course book, the manual offers the instructor material regarding practice and procedure in the Surrogate's Court and in the field of trusts and estates.

Wills, Trusts and Estate Administration

Syllabus for 8 week, 2 credit course

Text: <u>Wills, Trusts, and Estates, Essential Tools for the New York Paralegal</u>, 2nd edition, by Ilene S. Cooper

Date	Topic
Class 1	**Introduction to class** **Chapter 1 – no class discussion – use as reference** **Chapter 2 – The Laws of Intestacy** • **Introduction** • **Family Relationships** • **Per Stirpes, By Representation and Per Capita**
Class 2	**Chapter 2 – The Laws of Intestacy** • **The New York Statutory Formula** • **Petitioning for the Appointment of a Receiver** •
Class 3	**Chapter 3 – Status** • **Status as a Surviving Spouse** • **Adopted Children** • **Posthumous Children** • **Pretermitted Children** • **Non-Marital Children** • **Disqualification and Forfeiture**
Class 4	**Chapter 4 – The Elective Share Statute** • **Waiving the Elective Share** • **Procedure for Claiming the Elective Share** • **Computation of the Elective Share**
Class 5	**Test # 1**
Class 6	**Chapter 5 –Probate of Wills** • **The Requirements of Due Execution** • **Issues Involved in the Execution of Wills**

Date	Topic
Class 7	**Chapter 5 – Probate of Wills** • **Petitioning for Probate of a Decedent's Will** • **The Probate Petition** • **Appointment of an Executor**
Class 8	**Chapter 6 – Contested Probate Proceedings** • **Overview** • **Objections to Probate** • **Burden of Proof** • **Proof of Due Execution** • **Proof of Testamentary Capacity** • **Proof of Undue Influence** • **Confidential Relationships** • **Proof of Fraud**
Class 9	**Chapter 7 – Revocation of Wills** • **Requirements for Revocation** • **Physical Revocation** • **Codicils and Wills**
Class 10	**Test # 2**
Class 11	**Chapter 9 – Trusts** • **Essential Elements of an Express Trust** • **Interests in Trust** • **Types of Trusts** • **Amendment and Termination of Trusts**
Class 12	**Chapter 11 – Jurisdiction and Power of the Surrogate's Court** • **Subject Matter Jurisdiction** • **Personal Jurisdiction** • **Power of the Surrogate's Court** **Chapter 12 – Venue of Surrogate's Court Proceedings** • **A Question of Venue** • **Transfer of Venue**
Class 13	**Chapter 13 – Fiduciary Duties in Administering an Estate** • **Duties Prior to Probate** • **Marshalling Assets** • **Investment of Estate Property** • **Payment of Debts and Expenses**

Date	Topic
Class 14	**Chapter 13 – Fiduciary Duties in Administering an Estate** • **Decedent's Final Income Tax Return** • **Federal Estate Tax** • **New York Estate Tax** • **Fiduciary Income Tax**
Class 15	**Chapter 13 – Fiduciary Duties in Administering an Estate** • **Fiduciary Inventory** • **Satisfaction of Legacies and Bequests** • **Estate Accounting** • **Fiduciary Commissions** • **Legal Fees**
Class 16	• **Test # 4 or Final Exam**

Wills, Trusts and Estate Administration

Syllabus for 15 week, 3 credit course

Text: <u>Wills, Trusts, and Estates, Essential Tools for the New York Paralegal</u>, 2nd edition, by Ilene S. Cooper

Date	Topic
Class 1	**Introduction to class** **Chapter 1 – Essential Terms and Definitions**
Class 2	**Chapter 2 – The Laws of Intestacy** • **Introduction** • **Family Relationships** • **Per Stirpes, By Representation and Per Capita**
Class 3	**Chapter 2 – The Laws of Intestacy** • **The New York Statutory Formula** • **Petitioning for the Appointment of a Receiver** • **Review Administration Petition in Class OR Assign as Homework Project**
Class 4	**Chapter 3 – Status** • **Status as a Surviving Spouse** • **Review of Common Law Marriage** • **Divorce, Abandonment and Failure to Support** • **Adopted Children**
Class 5	**Chapter 3 – Status** • **Posthumous Children** • **Pretermitted Children** • **Non-Marital Children** • **Disqualification of Parent** • **Forfeiture**
Class 6	**Chapter 4 – The Elective Share Statute** • **Waiving the Elective Share** • **Procedure for Claiming the Elective Share**
Class 7	**Chapter 4 – The Elective Share** • **Computation of the Elective Share**

Date	Topic
Class 8	**Test # 1**
Class 9	**Chapter 5 –Probate of Wills** • **The Requirements of Due Execution** • **Nuncupative and Holographic Wills** • **Issues Involved in the Execution of Wills** • **Ancient Wills**
Class 10	**Chapter 5 – Probate of Wills** • **Petitioning for Probate of a Decedent's Will** • **Completion of a Probate Petition** • **Appointment of an Executor**
Class 11	**Chapter 6 – Contested Probate Proceedings** • **Overview** • **Objections to Probate** • **Burden of Proof** • **Proof of Due Execution** • **Proof of Testamentary Capacity** • **Proof of Undue Influence** • **Confidential Relationships** • **Proof of Fraud**
Class 12	**Chapter 7 – Revocation of Wills** • **Requirements for Revocation** • **Physical Revocation** • **Codicils and Wills**
Class 13	**Chapter 8 – Joint Wills and Mutual Wills** • **Definitions** • **Breach of Contract**
Class 14	**Test # 2**
Class 15	**Chapter 9 – Trusts** • **Essential Elements of an Express Trust** • **Interests in Trust** • **Types of Trusts** • **Amendment and Termination of Trusts**

Date	Topic
Class 16	**Chapter 10 – Gift Transactions** • **Intent** • **Delivery** • **Delivery** • **Acceptance** • **Gifts Causa Mortis**
Class 17	**Chapter 11 – Jurisdiction and Power of the Surrogate's Court** • **Subject Matter Jurisdiction** • **Personal Jurisdiction** • **Power of the Surrogate's Court**
Class 18	**Chapter 12 – Venue of Surrogate's Court Proceedings** • **A Question of Venue** • **Transfer of Venue**
Class 19	**Test # 3**
Class 20	**Chapter 13 – Fiduciary Duties in Administering an Estate** • **Duties Prior to Probate** • **Marshalling Assets** • **Investment of Estate Property** • **Payment of Debts and Expenses**
Class 21	**Chapter 13 – Fiduciary Duties in Administering an Estate** • **Decedent's Final Income Tax Return** • **Federal Estate Tax** • **New York Estate Tax** • **Fiduciary Income Tax**
Class 22	**Chapter 13 – Fiduciary Duties in Administering an Estate** • **Fiduciary Inventory** • **Satisfaction of Legacies and Bequests** • **Estate Accounting** • **Fiduciary Commissions** • **Legal Fees**
Class 23	**Chapter 14 – Ethical Issues** • **Ethical Standards for Paralegals** • **The Unauthorized Practice of Law** • **Preserving Client Confidences** • **Attorney/Beneficiary** • **Attorney/Fiduciary**

Date	Topic
Class 24	**Test # 4 or Final Exam**

Wills, Trusts and Estate Administration

Syllabus for 15 week, 3 credit course

Text: <u>Wills, Trusts, and Estates, Essential Tools for the New York Paralegal</u>, 2nd edition, by Ilene S. Cooper

Date	Topic
Class 1	**Introduction to class**
Class 2	**Chapter 1 – Essential Terms and Definitions**
Class 3	**Chapter 2 – The Laws of Intestacy** • **Introduction** • **Family Relationships**
Class 4	**Chapter 2 – The Laws of Intestacy** • **Per Stirpes, By Representation and Per Capita** • **The New York Statutory Formula**
Class 5	**Chapter 2 – The Laws of Intestacy** • **Petitioning for the Appointment of a Receiver** • **Review Administration Petition in Class OR Assign as Homework Project**
Class 6	**Chapter 3 – Status** • **Status as a Surviving Spouse** • **Review of Common Law Marriage** • **Divorce, Abandonment and Failure to Support**
Class 7	**Chapter 3 – Status** • **Adopted Children** • **Posthumous Children**
Class 8	**Chapter 3 – Status** • **Pretermitted Children** • **Non-Marital Children**
Class 9	**Chapter 3 – Status** • **Disqualification of a Parent** • **Forfeiture**
Class 10	**Test # 1**

Date	Topic
Class 11	**Chapter 4 – The Elective Share Statute** • **Waiving the Elective Share** • **Procedure for Claiming the Elective Share**
Class 12	**Chapter 4 – The Elective Share** • **Computation of the Elective Share**
Class 13	**Chapter 5 –Probate of Wills** • **The Requirements of Due Execution** • **Nuncupative and Holographic Wills**
Class 14	**Chapter 5 – Probate of Wills** • **Issues Involved in the Execution of Wills** • **Ancient Wills**
Class 15	**Petitioning for Probate of a Decedent's Will** • **Completion of a Probate Petition** • **Appointment of an Executor**
Class 16	**Test # 2**
Class 17	**Chapter 6 – Contested Probate Proceedings** • **Overview** • **Objections to Probate** • **Burden of Proof**
Class 18	**Chapter 6 – Contested Probate Proceedings** • **Proof of Due Execution** • **Proof of Testamentary Capacity** • **Proof of Undue Influence** • **Confidential Relationships** • **Proof of Fraud**
Class 19	**Chapter 7 – Revocation of Wills** • **Requirements for Revocation** • **Physical Revocation** • **Codicils and Wills**
Class 20	**Chapter 8 – Joint Wills and Mutual Wills** • **Definitions** • **Breach of Contract**
Class 21	**Test # 3**

Date	Topic
Class 22	**Chapter 9 – Trusts** • **Essential Elements of an Express Trust** • **Interests in Trust**
Class 23	**Chapter 9 – Trusts** • **Types of Trusts** • **Amendment and Termination of Trusts**
Class 24	**Chapter 10 – Gift Transactions** • **Intent** • **Delivery**
Class 25	**Chapter 10 – Gifts** • **Delivery** • **Acceptance** • **Gifts Causa Mortis**
Class 26	**Chapter 11 – Jurisdiction and Power of the Surrogate's Court** • **Subject Matter Jurisdiction**
Class 27	**Chapter 11 – Jurisdiction and Power of the Surrogate's Court** • **Personal Jurisdiction** • **Power of the Surrogate's Court**
Class 28	**Chapter 12 – Venue of Surrogate's Court Proceedings** • **A Question of Venue** • **Transfer of Venue**
Class 29	Test # 4
Class 30	**Chapter 13 – Fiduciary Duties in Administering an Estate** • **Duties Prior to Probate** • **Marshalling Assets**
Class 31	**Chapter 13 – Fiduciary Duties in Administering an Estate** • **Investment of Estate Property** • **Payment of Debts and Expenses**
Class 32	**Chapter 13 – Fiduciary Duties in Administering an Estate** • **Decedent's Final Income Tax Return** • **Federal Estate Tax** • **New York Estate Tax** • **Fiduciary Income Tax**

Date	Topic
Class 33	**Chapter 13 – Fiduciary Duties in Administering an Estate** • **Fiduciary Inventory** • **Satisfaction of Legacies and Bequests**
Class 34	**Chapter 13 – Fiduciary Duties in Administering an Estate** • **In Class Preparation and Review of an Estate Accounting**
Class 35	**Chapter 13 – Fiduciary Duties in Administering an Estate** • **In Class Preparation and Review of an Estate Accounting**
Class 36	**Chapter 13 – Fiduciary Duties in Administering an Estate** • **Fiduciary Commissions** • **Legal Fees**
Class 37	**Chapter 14 – Ethical Issues** • **Ethical Standards for Paralegals** • **The Unauthorized Practice of Law**
Class 38	**Chapter 14 – Ethical Issues** • **Preserving Client Confidences** • **Attorney/Beneficiary** • **Attorney/Fiduciary**
Class 39	**Class Review**
Class 40	**Test # 5 or Final Exam**

Chapter 1
Essential Terms and Definitions Utilized in Surrogate's Court Practice

Chapter Overview

Before embarking on a study of trusts and estates, it serves to provide the class with a bird's eye view of the Surrogate's Court—the number of Surrogate's Courts in the State, the number of Surrogate's sitting in each Court, Court personnel, and the departmental operation of the Court. To this extent, reference may be made to Appendix C, which is a listing of the Surrogate's Courts throughout the State.

There are fifty-three Surrogate's Courts in New York State, with one Surrogate sitting in each court, with the exception of the Surrogate's Court in New York County where there are two Surrogates. In addition to the Surrogate, the Surrogate's Court personnel generally consist of a Chief Clerk, a Deputy Chief Clerk, members of the Court's law department, consisting of the Law Secretary to Judge, Principal Court Attorneys-Referees, and Law Assistants, and Court employees, consisting of typists, intake clerks, and department heads.

The Surrogate's Court is typically divided into departments denoted by the type of proceeding which may be institute. Hence, there is a probate department, an administration department, an accounting department, a guardianship department, and a miscellaneous department. All proceedings which are submitted for filing should be sent to the department to which the proceeding pertains. Students should be cautioned that transmittal of papers to the law department will not speed the review process, and could, in fact, result in delay, as papers are re-routed to the correct department for considerations.

Questions regarding forms or intake should initially be directed to department clerks or department heads. If a difficult or complex question is involved, an appointment should be made with the department head, or if the question is legal in nature, by the attorney with whom the paralegal works and a member of the Court's law department.

Chapter One is principally designed to introduce students to terms commonly utilized in the area of trusts and estates. This topic serves as the subject of the first chapter of the course book so that familiarity with practical phrases and definitions will be bred at the outset of the course and developed throughout the term. Students, by the end of Chapter One, should have a basic understanding of such words as fiduciary, trust, will and codicil, as well as such phrases as testamentary trust, insolvent estate, and confidential relationship. Repeated use of the terms and phrases set forth in Chapter One should enhance this understanding.

Chapter One should also serve as a means of expanding the discussion of various concepts pertinent to case law, or to subjects addressed in other portions of the text, or perhaps, to subjects not addressed in the text at all but of practical interest.

The definitions in Chapter One reference provisions contained in the SCPA and the EPTL. Students should be informed that the term SCPA refers to the Surrogate's Court Procedure Act, and the term EPTL refers to the Estates, Powers and Trusts Law. The SCPA and the EPTL should be described to students as the essential statutory tool of Surrogate's Court practice and procedure. Its importance and use should not be underestimated. Students should be informed that they will rely on the statutes for the answers to their substantive and procedural questions related to the filed of trusts and estates—the EPTL being the substantive component of the statutes, and the SCPA being the procedural component.

Page 4. Confidential Relationship

The goal here should be to have the students think about the many relationships which may be considered fiduciary in nature and the circumstances under which a relationship may be deemed confidential in nature. Start by asking whether students can provide an example(s) of a fiduciary relationship and a confidential relationship. Have them consider the interrelationship between the parties in each example they offer. Then, discuss the following cases in order to insure the students' understanding.

In *Katzman v. Zion*, N.Y.L.J. Aug. 28, 1986 (Surrogate's Court Bronx County), the court enunciated the difference between a fiduciary relationship and confidential relationship, and found, with respect to the intervention of equity, that a fiduciary relationship exists as a matter of law, while a confidential relationship has to be determined as a matter of fact from the circumstances. The court described fiduciary relationships as including such formal legal relationships as directors and shareholders, guardian and ward, trustee and trust beneficiary, administrator and heirs, attorney and client, and principal and agent. By comparison, the court found that confidential relationships are not confined to any specific association or parties, but instead encompasses a broad spectrum of relations including moral, social, domestic, and/or merely personal ones in which one person reposes trust and confidence in another.

Matter of Evanchuk, 145 A.D.2d 559 (2d Dept. 1988), discussed the nature of a confidential relationship in the context of a contested probate proceeding.

On the issue of confidential relationships and undue influence, the decision in *Matter of Burke*, 82 A.D.2d 260 (2d Dept. 1981), should be discussed with the class. The devision is equally useful in demonstrating the factual analysis involved in determing the existence of confidential relationship.

Page 5. Eligibility to Receive Letters

The class should be referred to the provisions of SCPA Secs. 711 and 719, which provide grounds for revoking the appointment of a fiduciary once letters have been issued. On this topic, have the class consider whether hostility between the fiduciary and beneficiary(ies) of the estate is sufficient to revoke letters.

Page 6. Qualification of a Fiduciary

The students should recognize that a named executor will fail to qualify if he/she is ineligible to serve. Therefore, for example, if a named executor is a convicted felon, or an infant, he or she will not be eligible to serve and an administrator c.t.a. will be appointed to administer the estate. Caveat: If there is an alternate executor named in the will, he or she will have priority to a person who may be appointed administrator c.t.a.

Page 9. Preliminary Executor

Have the class consider whether a preliminary executor has unlimited authority to administer the estate once appointed. Point students to the provisions of SCPA Sec. 1412(3) which circumscribe the authority of the preliminary executor. Ask the class why these restrictions might be necessary during the pendency of a probate proceeding.

Reference should also be made to the provisions of SCPA Sec. 1412(5) which establishes the bond requirements of a preliminary executor. In particular, students should recognize that a preliminary executor will be required to post a bond unless the will expressly dispenses with the filing of a bond. Caveat: The Court, under such circumstances, may nevertheless exercise its discretion and require that a bond be posted.

Page 10. Temporary Administrator

Students should be asked to consider under what circumstances a temporary administrator would be appointed when there is a delay in the probate of a will. Generally, a preliminary executor is appointed in this instance. Are there cases where a preliminary executor may not be appointed? The discussion should cover the situation where the preliminary executor is charged with fraud or undue influence.

Practice Exercises

1. A person appointed to administer a small estate: **Voluntary Administrator**.

2. A supplement to a will, adding to, or altering its provisions, or confirming it in whole or in part: **Codicil.**

3. The fiduciary appointed where the office of administrator is vacant: **Administrator d.b.n.**

4. A testamentary disposition of real property: **Devise.**

5. A testamentary disposition to be taken out of a specified or identified property: **Demonstrative Disposition.**

6. A dispositive instrument written entirely in the hand of the testator, which is not executed in accordance with the statutory formalities prescribed by EPTL Sec. 3-2.1: **Holographic Will.**

7. A disposition of a specified or identified item of the testator's property: **Specific Disposition.**

8. A person appointed to administer the estate of a decedent who dies without a will: **Administrator.**

9. A person appointed to administer the estate of a decedent who dies without a will, domiciled in another state: **Ancillary Administrator.**

10. The person appointed when a named executor in a will fails to qualify or when the office of executor is vacant: **Administrator c.t.a.**

Questions to Consider

1. (a) Mr. Jones' daughter could raise the following grounds to object to her brother's petition to be appointed administrator of their father's estate:
   (i) that he is incompetent;
   (ii) that he is a non-domiciliary alien;
   (iii) that he is a felon; or
   (iv) that he is someone who does not possess the requisite qualifications required of a fiduciary by reason of substance abuse, dishonesty, improvidence, want of understanding, or that he is otherwise unfit to serve as administrator.
(b) Mr. Jones's infant daughter is not eligible to be appointed administrator.
(c) During the litigation, the court may appoint a temporary administrator.

2. The court should appoint a voluntary administrator to administer Susan's estate.

3. The court may appoint a preliminary executor during the probate contest to preserve the assets of the estate.

4. The court should appoint an administrator c.t.a.

Chapter 2
Intestate Administration

Chapter Overview

The purpose of this chapter is to introduce students to the laws of intestate succession, i.e. the manner in which property passes if a person dies without a will. Students should recognize that the laws of intestacy are a statutory scheme of inheritance, created by the State of New York for the passage of property. Essentially, therefore, when a person dies without a will, the State determines to whom and in what proportions his or her property will be distributed. The State also determines who is entitled to administer or to serve as the fiduciary of the estate, establishing a statutory priority among the decedent's intestate heirs.

While teaching this chapter, it is important to emphasize to the students that the laws of intestacy serve as the rudimentary building blocks for estate and trust administration and litigation. For example, an understanding of intestate succession is necessary to complete a probate petition, to understanding issues related to jurisdiction in probate, administration and accounting proceedings, and to the construction and interpretation of wills and trusts.

Page 13.

In discussing the implications of dying without a will, have students top to consider why it might be important to have a will. Is it important only to persons with sizeable estates? Is it important if a couple has children, but perhaps not a significant amount in the way of assets? Is it important in order to disinherit a relative, or to favor a friend? Does it facilitate gifts to charity? Is having a will more or less beneficial than having a revocable trust?

Page 15. Family Relationships and the Laws of Intestacy

Using the charts, in conjunction with the examples in the coursebook, have the class consider whether a relationship is lineal or collateral. First cousins, niece, grandchild? Great-grandparents? Make note to the class that New York does not permit more remote collateral heirs to inherit by intestacy from decedent's estate. Have the class consider the policy reasons for New York's law.

Page 16. Consanguinity

Lineal relationships, collateral relationships, and consanguinity are terms which interrelate. Both the decedent's lineal and collateral relatives are related to the decedent by consanguinity. Practice exercises related to determining the degree of consanguinity between the decedent and a survivor are useful in teaching the concept as well as reinforcing students' understanding of lineal and collateral relationships. In addition to the examples in the coursebook, students should be asked, as a classroom or homework assignment, to determine the degree of consanguinity between the decedent an dthe following:

- o Nieces and nephews
- o First cousins once removed
- o Great grandparents
- o Great grandnieces and great grandnephews
- o Great uncles and great aunts

Page 18. The Passage of Property by Intestacy

New York's laws on distribution "by representation" are derived from the Uniform Probate Code Sec. 2-103 and 2-106.

Although the New York laws of intestacy provide for distribution "by representation" and "per capita", students should still have a working understanding of the terms "per stirpes", since many testamentary instruments continue to direct that property be distributed in accordance with this method. Therefore, the examples in the coursebook concentrate upon a comparison between the passage of property "by representation" and "per stirpes".

Page 24. Exempt Property

The provisions of EPTS Sec. 5-3.1 have been liberally construed by the courts. (See *Matter of Williams*, 31 A.D. 617 (1898)). The language of the statute, when first enacted, indicated a desire of the Legislature to assist surviving spouses and minor children who lived in a rural environment. The only changes in the statute over the years have involved the age of children, and increases in the exemptions to reflect the changing economy.

Litigation has often arisen as to whether an asset constitutes exempt property. In *In re Estate of Queen*, N.Y.L.J., Feb. 27, 1998 (Surrogate's Court, Queens County), the decedent was survived by his wife, his brother, his sister, and his mother. His brother was appointed the executor of his estate. Upon his appointment, the executor commenced a proceeding to recover various items of personal property from the decedent's spouse. The decedent's spouse opposed the requested turnover claiming that the items in issue constituted exempt property and belonged to her pursuant to EPTL Sec. 5-3.1. The items included the following:

- o A MAC Performa computer software and diskettes
- o A MAC Performa personal computer and software
- o A Computer desk and chair
- o All clip files, research files, articles and stories used or produced by the decedent in his business
- o Video tapes of the decedent working as a news reporter
- o Audio tapes of the decedent doing Newsday commercials or other assignments as a News reporter

- o The audio tape used as the decedent's outgoing message on his telephone answering machine

The decedent's spouse moved for summary judgment declaring her to be the lawful owner of these items; the executor opposed and cross-moved for judgment declaring the estate to be the owner.

In determining the matter, the court noted that while the burden of proving that an asset constitutes exempt property resets with the person claiming it as such, the law is liberally construed in favor of the surviving spouse. With this and the statutory provisions of EPTL Sec. 5-3.1 in mind, the court determined that the MAC Performa computer hardware, including the monitor, modem, CPU, printer, mouse, and scanner, and the computer desk and chair were exempt property which the spouse was entitled to retain. The court reached this determination despite the fact that the computer housed material that was wholly business-related, concluding that so long as it was located in the decedent's home, it constituted "household furniture used in or about the house" pursuant to EPTL Sec. 5.3.1(a)(1). The court reached a similar result with respect to the videotapes, disks, and software, holding that they were specifically exempt pursuant to the provisions of EPTL Sec. 5-3.1(a)(2).

On the other hand, the court held that there was no specific statutory exemption for audiotapes, clip files, research files, and articles and stories of the decedent, and therefore, created the executor's request for judgment directing that they be turned over to the estate.

In examining this decision and the provisions of the exempt property statute have the students consider the following:
- o The public policy underlying the statute
- o The reason(s), if any, why the decedent's jewelry has been omitted from the statute as exempt property, while the decedent's clothing is specifically made exempt
- o The policy behind the provision which authorizes the use of otherwise exempt property (i.e. money or other personal property) to satisfy the reasonable funeral expenses of the decedent, where the assets are otherwise insufficient to satisfy those expenses.

Page 29. Contents of Petition

Remind students that in setting forth the address of the petitioner, the decedent, or the decedent's distributes, a post office box address will not be sufficient. A street number and street name is required. Additionally, students should be informed that a hospital address should not be listed as the decedent's domiciliary address at death, although a nursing home may constitute a decedent's domiciliary address, depending upon the circumstances.

Page 30. Filing Checklist

Students should note that where a distributee predeceases the decedent leaving issue, a death certificate for that distribute may be required.

With respect to item #6 on the list, students should be referred to the provisions of Uniform Court Rule (UCR) 207.16(d) for a guide as to the sources of information to be utilized in making a diligent seach.

Page 30. Disqualification

A spouse may also be disqualified if it is established that he or she is not the surviving spouse of the decedent. This often occurs under circumstances where there is a claim of common law marriage.

Practice Exercises

1-2. (a) On January 10, 1993 the entire estate would go to the issue by representation, so the estate would be distributed as follows:
(i) the surviving child would get 1/3.
(ii) each surviving grandchild would get 1/6.
(iii) each great grandchild would get 1/9.

(b) If the decedent had died on June 10, 1992, the entire estate would go to the issue per stirpes, so that the estate would be distributed as follows:
(1) the surviving child would get 1/3.
(ii) each surviving grandchild would get 1/6.
(iii) the great grandchild who is an only child would get 1/6, and the great grandchildren who are siblings would each get 1/12.

3. The decedent was survived by more than one child or issue of a child, so the spouse would receive 1/3 of the net estate. The balance would go to the issue per stirpes so that the rest of the estate would be distributed as follows:
(i) the surviving child would get 1/3 of the remaining net estate, or 2/9 of the total net estate (1/3 times 2/3 = 2/9).
(ii) the grandchild who is an only child would also get 1/3 of the remaining net estate, or 2/9 of the total net estate (1/3 times 2/3 = 2/9).
(iii) the grandchildren who are siblings would each get 1/6 of the remaining net estate, or 1/9 of the total net estate (1/6 times 2/3 = 2/18 = 1/9).

(a) The estate available for distribution would be $500,000 less $50,000 ($10,000 debts plus $30,000 exempt property plus $10,000 funeral expenses) = $450,000. This would be distributed as follows:
(i) the surviving spouse would get $150,000.
(ii) the surviving child would get $100,000.
(iii) the grandchild who is an only child would get $100,000.

(iv) the grandchildren who are siblings would each get $50,000.

4. The estate would be distributed ½ to the cousins on the decedent's paternal side and ½ to the cousins on the decedent's maternal side. Each of the paternal cousins would receive 1/6 of the estate (1/2 times 1/3) and each of the maternal cousins would receive ¼ of the estate (1/2 times 1/2).

Questions to Consider

2. The amount of the administrator's bond would be $30,000.

3. The decedent's aunt would be entitled to priority in receiving letters of administration because she is closer to him in degrees of consanguinity and would be entitled to receive a larger share of his estate than the three cousins. If all of the distributees were ineligible to serve, the Surrogate's Court would appoint a Public Administrator.

Chapter 3
Status

Chapter Overview

The purpose of this chapter is to introduce students to the various aspects of status: the different relationships integral to status, and the affect of status upon a person's inheritance rights as well as right to serve as fiduciary of an estate. Status thus plays an important role in estate administration and estate litigation.

Indeed, many a courtroom has been witness to disputes regarding a person's claim to be a spouse, or a non-marital child, or an adopted child of a decedent. Equally true, many an estate administration has been complicated by efforts to ascertain the existence of the decedent's distributes, be they non-marital children, or otherwise.

A clear example of just this type of administrative dilemma may be found in *In re Estate of Alao*, N.Y.L.J., Mar. 19, 2002 (Surrogate's Court, Kings County). It would serve to discuss this opinion with the class at this juncture in order to illustrate the extent to which the issue of status plays in the administration of an estate, and more specifically, its distribution.

At issue in *Alao* was the claim of the decedent's marital children that they were entitled to inherit the decedent's entire estate. Although the court determined that the claimants were in fact the decedent's children, the record also demonstrated that the decedent had at least one non-marital child. As such, the court held that before their distributive share of the claimants could be fixed and paid to them they had to demonstrate that there were not other children of the deceased, or, if there were other children, the number of such children. The court opined: "In order to demonstrate their distributive rights, claimants must establish: (1) their relationship to the decedent, (2) the absence of any person with a closer relationship to the decedent, and (3) the maximum number of persons having the same degree of relationship to the decedent . . . Claimants who fail to offer evidence to exclude the existence of persons who would have an equal right to share in the estate, fail to establish their rights as distributes . . . ".

It should be pointed out to the class that the party asserting a claim against an estate in order to establish inheritance rights has the burden of doing so by clear and convincing evidence. This is made clear throughout the discussion in this chapter. *See, e.g.,* the discussion of common law marriage at page **37.**

Provisions of Domestic Relations Law Sec. 117 are not on hand. It is therefore recommended that copies of DRL Sec. 117 be made and distributed to the class before embarking upon any discussion of the topic.

It is also recommended that examples, in addition to those provided in the coursebook, be given to the class in order to further develop their understanding of DRL Sec. 117. For this purpose, consider the following problems:

(1) M and F had 2 children. M and F divorced. M had custody of C1 and F had custody of C2. M remarried and her husband H2 adopted C1 with M's consent. F did not remarry. F dies intestate on September 1, 1995.

Page 38. After discussion of the Benjamin case

Proof of the parties conduct is essential in establishing a common law marriage. While conduct in the common law state is the primary determinant, the students should note that consideration is also given to the parties' conduct in New York. Although this evidence is not as determinative of the issue, it has been held that "where the visit the common law state is brief, of necessity, the parties activities at their domicile must be analyzed to determine their intention." *See In re Estate of Libertini*, N.Y.L.J. Nov. 2, 1999 (Surrogate's Court, New York County).

The foregoing point is evidenced by the decision in *Renshaw v. Heckler,* 787 F.2d 50 (1986). This decision is equally of interest in demonstrating that a party's status not only can have an impact upon his/her inheritance rights as a distributee or beneficiary under a will, but also to death benefits under employment plans and social security.

As defined by the court, the issue in *Renshaw*, was whether the Secretary of Health and Human Services and the District Court erred in determining that under Pennsylvania law, the plaintiff, Edith Renshaw, was not the common law wife of the decedent and therefore not entitled to inherit widow's insurance benefits under the Social Security Act. In reversing the determination of the District Court, the Second Circuit concluded that the parties had entered a valid common law marriage under the laws of Pennsylvania and that the decedent's widow was entitled to the death benefits which she claimed as his spouse.

In reaching this result, the court found that the parties' conduct while in Pennsylvania and elsewhere was sufficient to support a finding that they considered themselves to be husband and wife and had entered into a valid common law marriage under Pennsylvania law. In particular, the court noted that while there was no evidence of a present intent to create a marriage in Pennsylvania, the uncontroverted proof as to the parties' twenty-one year relationship, and the fact that all their relatives, friends, and acquaintances had assumed they were married, negated the possibility of any fraudulent claim on plaintiff's part as to her status as the decedent's spouse.

Refer the class, as well, to the decision in *Tornese v. Tornese*, N.Y.L.J., Nov. 28, 1995 (Surrogate's Court, Westchester County), where the court, in finding that the parties had entered a valid common law marriage in Pennsylvania, relied, *inter alia*, upon proof that the parties, while in New York, bought property and made investments as husband

and wife, banked as husband and wife, maintained club memberships, obtained insurance as husband and wife, celebrated wedding anniversaries, and filed tax returns as husband and wife.

Page 43. After Form of Acknowledgment

The form of acknowledgment is set forth in Real Property Law Sec. 309-a, effective September 1, 1999. It should be emphasized that the form as it appears is essential to the validity of an agreement containing a waiver of spousal rights. Failure to comply with the language in the form can result in the agreement being declared void or unenforceable.

This point may be illustrated through a discussion of the decision in *Paul v. Paul*, N.Y.L.J., Apr. 23, 2002 (Sup. Court, Kings County), wherein the court held a separation agreement void on the grounds that the acknowledgment failed to conform to the form of acknowledgment established by Real Property Law Sec. 309-a.

Page 43. Matter of Greiff

After discussing the decision in *Greiff*, ask the students whether the law which was applied in the case should also apply in probate cases where the stronger, more dominant party is the principal beneficiary under the decedent's will. Should the more dominant party have the burden of establishing that the will under which he/she benefits was fair and voluntary? Questions of this nature will serve as useful prelude to Chapter 6, Contested Probate Proceedings.

Page 44. After discussion of Abandonment

After discussing the elements of abandonment, have the students consider that the "departure" may be made by the decedent or the surviving spouse. When a decedent is caused to depart from the household, thereby leaving the surviving spouse, an abandonment by the surviving spouse may still be found. This type of abandonment is known as constructive abandonment and is represented by conduct so intolerable by the surviving spouse that it results in the decedent's justifiable departure from the marital home.

Page 46. Inheritance Rights of adopted Children

The inheritance rights of adopted children, both by will and pursuant to the laws of intestacy, often causes confusion for students, particularly where the C1 inherit from F? Yes- DRL 117 (1)(e)

b)   Can C2 inherit from F? Yes.

Assume M then dies.

c)   Can 1 inherit from M? Yes- DRL 117(1)(d)

d)   Can C2 inherit from M? Yes- C2 was not adopted.

(2) Suppose in the above example, C1 died on September 1, 1995?

      (a)   Can M inherit from C1? Yes- DRL 117(1)(d)

      (b)   Can H2 inherit from C1? Yes- DRL 117(1)(c)

      (c)   Can F inherit from C1? No- DRL 117(1)(a)

      (d)   Can C2 inherit from C1? Yes- DRL 117(1)(d)

Page 51. After-Born Children (after discussion of the Wilkins case)

The class should be made aware that where a claim is made by a non-marital child to share in the estate of a deceased father, issues of paternity may arise. Accordingly, the court in *Matter of Wilkins*, 180 Misc.2d 568 (1999) held: "It would appear to be consistent with this tend and with the precedents tying applicability of EPTL Sec. 5-3.2...to legitimation under EPTL Sec.4-1.2...to hold that non-marital child who establishes his or her status under EPTL Sec.4-1.2(a)(2)(C) should also be recognized as an after-born child under EPTL Sec.5-3.2." Ask the class whether the same concerns regarding EPTL Sec.4-1.2 arise where the decedent is the child's mother? This will serve as a useful means of introducing the class to the provisions of EPTL Sec. 4-1.2.

Page 52. Non-Marital Children

Ensure that the class recognizes that the order of filiation must be entered during the father's lifetime. Where an order of filiation is entered after the decedent's death, it is insufficient to establish paternity pursuant to the provisions of EPTL 4-1.2(a)(2)(A).

Page 54. The provisions of EPTL 4-1.2(a)(2)(C)

This section is often used as a catch all provision by which a court may consider evidence of paternity which does not fall within the category of the other statutory sections governing paternity. Thus in *In re Estate of Bonano*, N.Y.L.J., Apr. 22, 2002 (Surrogate's Court, New York County), the court utilized the results of posthumously obtained DNA test as evidence relevant to the issue of paternity pursuant to EPTL Sec. 4-1.2(a)(2)(C). Currently, the results of such tests are inadmissible pursuant to the provisions of EPTL Sec. 4-1.2(a)(2)(D). *See* discussion of *In re Estate of DeLuca*, N.Y.L.J., Jan. 5, 1998 (Surrogate's Court, Suffolk County), in the course book.

Page 55. Disqualification of a Parent

The burden of proving the disqualification of a parent either on the ground of abandonment or non-support is on the party asserting it. *See Matter of Clark*, 119 A.D.2d 947 (3d Dept. 1986).

Page 57. Forfeiture

The rule of forfeiture raises some very interesting issues regarding quantum of proof and double jeopardy. Interesting discussion may be generated with the following questions: (1) If A is convicted in a criminal proceeding of first degree manslaughter, can a forfeiture automatically be adjudicated in the Surrogate's Court? The answer to this question is "yes". Since the quantum of proof in a criminal case is beyond a reasonable doubt, a standard which is much higher than in a civil case, a forfeiture is automatic; (2) If A is found not guilty in a criminal proceeding, can a forfeiture be adjudicated in the Surrogate's Court? The answer to this question is "yes". There is no double jeopardy, since one proceeding is a criminal proceeding, and the second proceeding is a civil proceeding; (3) If A is found guilty of manslaughter in the second degree in a criminal proceeding, should an adjudication of forfeiture in the Surrogate's Court based on the criminal conviction await the end-result of the appeal, if there is one, of the criminal case? The answer to this question is "yes." Since the appellate process could result in a reversal of the criminal conviction, an adjudication of forfeiture in the Surrogate's Court based upon the criminal conviction would be premature. *See In re Estate of Scott*, N.Y.L.J., Mar. 27, 2001 (Surrogate's Court, Nassau County).

Practice Exercises

1. (a) C1 cannot inherit from M, according to the provisions of New York Domestic Relations Law, section 117(1).
(b) If Mr. Smith is C1's uncle, C1 can inherit from M because, according to New York Domestic Relations Law, section 117(1)(e):
(i) M died after August 31, 1987;
(ii) M was a descendant of C1's natural grandparent; and
(iii) the person who adopted C1 is a descendant of C1's natural grandparent.
(c) C can inherit from Mr. Smith according to the provisions of New York Domestic Relations Law section 117(1)(c).

2. Yes, according to New York Domestic Relations Law section 117(1)(c), the niece can inherit from D.

3. The after born child is a pretermitted child and will be entitled to inherit from T's estate. T's specific limit to his two living children did not affect his third child, who will inherit what would have been the child's intestate share. Under intestacy laws the wife is entitled to $50,000 plus ½ of the net estate, and the rest is to go to the issue by representation. Therefore, the third child would receive an amount equal to 1/3 of the remaining net estate.

Questions to Consider

1. (a) Yes, C1 and C2 can inherit as part of the class gift.
(b) Yes, F's child with his second wife can inherit as part of the class gift.

2. Sally can raise the following arguments to invalidate the post nuptial agreement: Sam has more assets and is much more financially savvy than Sally, Sam has more education and financial training than Sally, Sam convinced Sally to sign the agreement, Sam's attorney represented both Sam and Sally, and the agreement was signed in a very informal setting which gave Sally no chance to review or negotiate the agreement.

3. It is not clear that Sam can inherit from B. In order to establish paternity for purposes of inheritance, a DNA test must have been conducted during the lifetime of the decedent. Surrogates will accept posthumous DNA test results if the father of the child has openly and notoriously acknowledged the child to be his own. Unfortunately for Sam, even though his father loved him privately, he was cold publicly, and never acknowledged Sam as his son, so it is doubtful that the posthumous test will be accepted to prove paternity for inheritance purposes.

4. The third child is not entitled to share in the bequest because his father made other arrangements for this child by creating the totten trust.

Chapter 4
The New York Elective Share Statute

Chapter Overview

The elective share statute is one of the most important and one of the most complex statutes which students will have to tackle. While conceptually, students will find the statute easy to understand, calculating the elective share often proves difficult. Plan on several hours of class time in order to teach the elective share, welcome questions, and provide as many examples and hypotheticals as possible. Repetition will prove effective.

Before discussing the provisions of EPTL Sec. 5-1.1-A have the class consider the legislative motives for expanding the scope of the elective share statute. This cold provide some interesting discussion respecting women's rights and social equality. The New York legislature had two main motives in making the changes from the former EPTL Sec. 5-1.1 to the present EPTL 5-1.1-A. "First, it intended to establish greater consistency between the elective share rules and New York's equitable distribution of marital property on divorce....[Equitable distribution] reflects a legislative conclusion that married individuals form an unspoken marital agreement in which each spouse possesses a half interest in all property nominally acquired by and titled in the sole name of either partner during the marriage...Secondly, the Legislature wanted to delete from the elective share provisions those aspects that reflected an earlier male-dominated belief in the inability of women to manage their own financial affairs." Hirschson, Linda B., and McCaffrey, Carlyn S., "New York's New Spousal Elective Share Law- What the Estate Planner Needs to Know", Trusts and Estates Newsletter, New York State Bar Association, p. 5 (Spring, 1993)

Page 64. Persons who may elect: surviving spouse

The elective share is available to a surviving spouse who has entered into a common law marriage with the decedent. *Matter of Pecorino*, 407 N.Y.S.2d 550 (2d Dept. 1978)

Page 64. Persons who may elect

Is a party a surviving spouse within the dictates of the statute where a divorce action between the decedent and survivor was resolved prior to death by stipulation, but a judgment of divorce was not signed? When does a divorce action become final so as to extinguish a surviving spouse's right to elect? In *In re Mirizzi*, N.Y.L.J., Mar. 27, 2001 (Surrogate's Court, Richmond County), the court held that under the circumstances the issues raised in the divorce had been resolved and the entry of a judgment of divorce was a mere ministerial act. Thus, the court determined that the parties were divorced and that the respondent was not entitled to inherit as a surviving spouse.

While on this subject, have the class consider whether an attorney-in-fact should be given the power to exercise a right of election.

Page 65. Filing and Service of Notice of Election : The Six Month Period

Note the exception to this rule: When a probate decree is vacated, the time to file a notice of election does not begin to run from the time letters were granted under that decree, because the decree is revoked in its entirety and the fiduciary appointment is void. *Matter of Latowitzky*, 56 Misc.2d 916 (1968) However, the two year limitation might nevertheless affect the outcome. Accordingly, in order to avoid the loss of the right, the surviving spouse should consider filing the notice with the named executor, if there is one, before the expiration of two years, even if there is a possibility of the probate decree being revoked.

Page 67. Default in Electing

An interesting opinion on this subject was rendered by the Bronx County Surrogate in *In re Yearwood*, N.Y.L.J., Mar. 8, 1995. In that case, the court was asked to determine whether a spouse could be relieved of a default under circumstances where the petition requesting that relief was filed shortly before the twelve month period had expired, but the interested parties were not notified of the of the proceeding until after the expiration of the period. The court held that the twelve month time limitation referred solely to the time within which the petition had to be filed and not to any other event. Quite logically, the court determined that if more than the filing of the petition was required "the spouse would be left to the mercy of the court because it would not be known either how long it might take the court to review the petition to determine whether notification had to be given to other parties, and if notification was required, how long it might take to effectuate the notification directed by the court." *Id.* at 27.

When discussing the provisions of EPTL Sec. 5-1.1-A(d)(2), the class should be made aware that in addition to complying with the statutory requirements, a surviving spouse must demonstrate reasonable cause for the delay in filing the election timely. Reasonable cause may exist, for example, where it is shown that the spouse's failure to timely elect was due to a limited ability to understand English (*see Matter of Lamash*, 8 Misc.2d 544 (1941)), or where it is shown that the surviving spouse mistakenly believed the estate was small. *See Matter of Crary*, 283 A.D. 760 (3d Dept. 1954)

Page 70. Waiver

A proper acknowledgment is essential to the validity of a waiver or release of an elective share. The class should be forewarned that the failure of an acknowledgment to comply with the statutory requirements may result in a waiver being declared invalid. On the other hand, in *In re Estate of Greenstein*, N.Y.L.J., Jun. 2, 1994 (Surrogate's Court, Nassau County), the court addressed two irregularities in an acknowledgment which it found were not fatal to its validity. The first such irregularity was the failure of the acknowledgment to mention the county in which it was taken. Referring to the provisions of RPL Secs. 298, 303 and 306, the court concluded that an acknowledgment within the State of a conveyance of real property situated in the State, may be made at any place within the State by a notary public so long as there is an oral declaration by the signer of the document, and an attestation by the notary of the declaration and identity of the signer. Hence, the court found that the omission was not a defect which would invalidate the acknowledgment. Furthermore, the court held that although there was a disparity between the date the agreement was signed and the date of the acknowledgment, there is no requirement that the acknowledgment of an agreement be made simultaneously or contemporaneously with its execution.

Practice Exercises

1. a. Step 1 – calculate the value of the net estate subject to the elective share:

$250,000 = value of estate
+   0 = intestate property
+100,000 = testamentary substitutes
$350,000 = gross estate subject to elective share
- 25,000 = debts and expenses
$325,000 = net estate subject to elective share

b. Step 2 – calculate the greater of $50,000 or 1/3 of the net estate; 1/3 = $108,333.33. Since $108,333.33 is greater than $50,000, the elective share is $108,333.33.

2. a. Step 1 – calculate the value of the net estate subject to the elective share:
$1,600,000 = value of estate
+   0 = intestate property
+   150,000 = totten trust = testamentary substitute
+   250,000 = joint bank account during marriage = testamentary substitute
$2,000,000 = gross estate subject to elective share

Note: - joint account is totally included since he contributed 100% of funds.
         - pension is not included since he designated beneficiary prior to 1992.
         - life insurance is not included.

$2,000,000
-   350,000 = debts and expenses
$ 650,000 = net estate subject to elective share

b. Step 2 – calculate the greater of $50,000 or 1/3 of the net estate subject to the elective share; 1/3 = $216,666.66. Since $216,666.66 is greater than $50,000, $216,666.66 is the gross elective share.

c. Step 3 – subtract any dispositions by will:
 $216,666.66
- 200,000.00
$ 16,666.66 = elective share

3. a. Step 1 – calculate the value of the net estate subject to the elective share:
 $ 750,000 = value of estate
    225,000 = testamentary substitute - house (after 1992 so presume each contributed ½)
    125,000 = testamentary substitute - totten trust
    225,000 = testamentary substitute – gift to brother
$1,325,000 = gross estate subject to elective share
$1,325,000
-   150,000 = debts and expenses
$1,175,000 = net estate subject to elective share

b. Step 2 – calculate the greater of $50,000 or 1/3 of the net estate subject to the elective share; 1/3 = 391,666.66. Since $391,666.66 is greater than $50,000 is the gross elective share.

c. Step 3 – subtract any dispositions by will = $0.00 so elective share = $391.666.66.

Questions to Consider

1. The decedent's spouse should file a notice of election in writing. She should serve the notice either personally or by mail on the temporary executor, and should file the original of the notice, together with proof of service of process, with the Surrogate's Court that issued the temporary letters. If two years have elapsed since the decedent's death, it is possible that the Surrogate's Court could relieve the spouse of her default under the law of Rosenkranz. In that case, the court relieved the surviving spouse from a default to exercise the elective share even though 40 months had passed since the date of death, when the will had still not been admitted to probate, even though preliminary letters had been issued.

2. In order to ensure that Jane waives her right to an elective share in Tom's estate, she should do so in writing, subscribed by her, and acknowledged in the manner required for the recording of deeds. The best vehicle for a waiver prior to marriage would be a prenuptial agreement.

3. The arguments that can be raised for Sarah are:
(i) Sarah was unable to care for John, so she did not let him go voluntarily;
(ii) Sarah had to move to California to be cared for by her son, so her departure was not voluntary;
(iii) John consented to Sarah's move; and
(iv) Sarah intended to return.

The arguments that can be raised against Sarah are:
(i) Sarah left John to go to California
(ii) Sarah's move was not justified by John's conduct;
(iii) Sarah's move was without John's consent; and
(iv) Sarah did not intend to return.

Chapter 5
Probate of Wills

Chapter Overview

Understanding the statutory requirements for due execution is essential for the trusts and estates paralegal. Proof of due execution is required for the admission of a will to probate, and where objections to probate are filed, compliance with the statutory requirements must be proven at trial.

Instruction of the material contained in Chapter Five may be enhanced through practical application; for example, demonstrating a will execution ceremony, distributing sample will forms, and having the class complete a probate petition.

In order to introduce the class to this subject, ask who in the class has a will and why they believe it is or is not important to have a will. Introduce the class to the concept of a trust, or more particularly, a revocable trust. Ask the class whether they think a revocable trust will be effective in avoiding probate or administration if there are assets which have not been transferred into the trust? If assets remain outside the trust at the time of the grantor's death, these assets will be distributed either pursuant to the terms of the decedent's will, or pursuant to the laws of intestacy.

Page 85.   The Requirements of Due Execution

Begin by asking the class why they believe the statutory requirements in the execution of a will are necessary? Is it beneficial for the testator? Beneficial to the testator's heirs? Should precautions, in addition to the statutory requirements be taken? Under what circumstances? These questions and others like them will activate class discussion on the subject.

At this juncture, it may be useful to have the students conduct a mock will execution ceremony. Bring a sample will into class which includes space for the testator's signature, an attestation clause, and a self-proving affidavit. Select a student to act as the lawyer supervising the execution, select three student witnesses, and select a student to serve as the testator. Once the players are assembled, provide the students with an overview of the statutory formalities, presumptions of due execution which follow when a will execution is attorney-supervised, and when the will has an attestation clause. Discuss with the students the importance of the attesting witnesses. Inform the students that the selection of good attesting witnesses, i.e. witnesses whose testimony will be especially persuasive in court, will be especially important when a will contest is likely.

Guide the students through the will execution ceremony. Emphasize the importance of counting the pages of the will before the ceremony begins, and stapling the will before it is signed. If a will is not stapled at the time of execution, the door is left open for accusations to be made that it is a fraudulent document- - the concept being that pages were inserted after it was signed. Often times, accusations of this nature will also be avoided by having the testator initial the margin of each page in addition to signing at the end of the instrument.

Once the testator has signed the instrument at the end, ask the students whether the witnesses should simply sign as witnesses, or whether the attestation clause should be read aloud. Have the students understand that the attestation clause should be read aloud to insure that the witnesses understand the significance of their serving as attesting witnesses.

Once the attesting witnesses have signed the will, have them sign the self-proving Affidavit or SCPA 1406 Affidavit which follows the will. Point out that this Affidavit avoids having to locate the attesting witnesses at the time of the testator's death, except in the case where their examination is sought, as may be the case when the will is contested.

Upon the completion of the will execution ceremony, ask the students where the original will should be kept. Is it a good idea that it be left with the testator? Other than with the attorney-draftsman, where else can the will be safeguarded?

At this juncture, ask the students how many of the statutory requirements were fulfilled during the course of the will execution ceremony.

Page 87.   The End of the Instrument

An interesting case which addressed the question of what constitutes "the end" of the instrument for due execution purposes is *In re Estate of Phillips*, N.Y.L.J., July 28, 1995 (Surrogate's Court, Bronx County). In *Phillips,*, the testator signed the instrument, the attestation clause followed the printed names of he witnesses, which were not in their hand, then appeared, and on the page preceding the testator's signature, the witnesses signed the SCPA1406 Affidavit.

The court found that the will had been duly executed and that the attesting witnesses signed their names at the end of the instrument. In reaching this result, the court noted that it made no difference whether the signature of the testator appeared above or below those of the attesting witnesses and the "end" of the will is the end of the dispositive language rather than a particular physical spot. Moreover, where the self-proving affidavit is attached to the rest of the instrument, it is as much a part of the will as the attestation clause.

Page 87.   In the Presence of Witnesses

In *In re Estate of Acosta*, N.Y.L.J., Jan. 10, 1995 (Surrogate's Court, New York County), the court was presented with the issue of whether a witness may affix his/her signature to the will after the testator is dead. The will was signed by the testator in the presence of the witnesses one hour before her died. Although they observed the testator sign the instrument, the witnesses did not immediately sign their names as witnesses, thinking they had to have their signatures notarized. While the witnesses signed their names to the instrument within thirty days of each other, they did so after the testator died. The court held that while the provisions of EPTL Sec. 3-3.2 do not expressly require the testator to be alive when the witnesses sign, in similar situations courts have held that the authority of the witnesses to sign terminates on the testator's death. The court opined that perhaps post-death signing by the witnesses would be sustained where an unexpected event interrupts the will execution ceremony, but in the case before it, no such event took place. Accordingly, the court found that the will had not been duly executed and denied probate.

Page 89. (Just before Nuncupative Will)

Reference may also be made to the decision in *Matter of Miele*, N.Y.L.J., Aug. 28, 1997 (Surrogate's Court, Westchester County), where the court found that the circumstances surrounding execution gave rise to an inference of publication in compliance with the statutory formalities. These circumstances revealed that when the decedent was asked by one of the attesting witnesses whether she knew what she was signing she nodded her head indicating that she did and then signed the instrument in front of the two witnesses.

Page 89. Nuncupative and Holographic Wills

Although nuncupative and holographic wills are recognized in New York, they are rarely the subject of a probate proceeding. Therefore, they should be briefly discussed, to the extent of pointing out to the class the rationale for legislative recognition of these types of wills, and ensuring the class understands the distinction between a holographic will, and a handwritten will which is not holographic.

Page 99. Mistake

When discussing the issue of a scrivener's error, it may prove interesting to the class to know that an attorney-draftsman cannot be sued by the beneficiaries of an estate for harm caused by professional negligence, unless the beneficiary can establish that counsel's malpractice was the result of fraud, collusion, or malicious acts. *Rationale:* the beneficiaries are not in privity with the attorney-draftsman. *See Conti v. Polizzotto*, N.Y.L.J. July 23, 1996 (Supreme Court, Kings County)

Page 99. Ancient Wills

To be compared with the result in *Kassover* is the decision in *In re Estate of Drew*, N.Y.L.J. Dec. 26, 1990 (Surrogate's Court, Bronx County), where the court denied probate of a will propounded as an ancient document where there was evidence of removal and replacement of staples, holding that the proponent had failed to satisfy the "unsuspicious nature" prong of the ancient document rule.

Page 102. Filing Checklist

A practice exercise in completing a probate petition will prove helpful in determining whether the class understands how to complete the form, and will familiarize the class with the specifics of the form. It should be noted that despite a Uniform Probate Petition form, some Surrogates continue to use their own forms, and/or require information in addition to that required in the form.

Page 102. Necessary Parties

The jurisdictional component of the probate petition is one of the most important elements. Failure to obtain jurisdiction over all necessary parties will result in a decree which will not be binding on the parties who were not served. Again, practice exercises will prove helpful and reinforcing.

Questions to Consider

1. The matters to be considered in determining the validity of the mark as T's signature are (a) whether T intended that the mark be her signature, and (b) whether the attestation clause mentions that the entire will was read aloud to T and that she signed by placing an X on the will.

2. This will and codicil should not be admitted to probate. They could be considered ancient and so would be admissible if they were unsuspicious. However these instruments are suspicious. They include many changes, the amendment was signed but not witnessed, there were handwritten changes in a different ink than that used to sign the will, and a typed insertion in darker ribbon that that used to type will.

3. The court can dispense with testimony of attesting witness if they are dead, out of state, incompetent, or cannot be located within the state after a due diligence search, or cannot be examined due to their physical or mental condition. This will can still be admitted for probate upon the testimony of the attesting witness who has been examined without any further proof. The will is also presumed valid because its preparation was supervised or prepared by attorney, and also because it is an ancient document that does not appear suspicious.

4. (a) The friend not entitled to the bequest. Under EPTL 3-3.2(a)(2), a disposition to a witness/beneficiary is effective if there were still two other witnesses at the time of the execution and attestation who received no beneficial disposition, unless will cannot be proved without testimony of the witness/beneficiary. In this case, the testimony of the secretary and friend will be needed, so the disposition is void.

(b) The result would be different if 1406 affidavits had been signed and affixed to the instrument because then the testimony of the friend would not be necessary and the disposition would be valid.

5. According to SPCA 1403, the necessary parties would be:

the son and daughter – as distributes of the decedent;
the two grandchildren, his brother and Cornell University because they would all get less under the 1998 will, and are therefore adversely affected.

6. A preliminary executor can sell the real property if he or she has the written permission of the beneficiary. In this case, the son has indicated that he does not want the real property, so with his consent it could be sold.

Chapter 6
Contested Probate Proceedings

Chapter Overview

A contested probate proceeding is the most frequently encountered litigation in the Surrogate's Court. Hence, the subject serves as a separate chapter of the book.

In addition to introducing the students to forms of pleadings in the Surrogate's Court, and the basis for filing objections to the propounded will, this chapter can also serve as a means of reviewing prior chapters of the book dealing with, for example, such subjects as intestacy, SCPA Sec. 1404 examinations, and status. Take advantage of this chapter for this purpose in order to reinforce the students' understanding of these concepts.

Furthermore, when teaching this chapter, have the students think about how to prepare a contested probate proceeding for trial- - from the perspective of the proponent of the will and the objectant to the will. What information will be relevant? What discovery devices can be utilized to obtain the information? What presumptions will assist in satisfying a party's burden of proof? What witnesses are needed? Will an expert witness be necessary? What documents are needed? Are medical authorizations necessary? And so forth. While a paralegal will not be responsible for strategizing a case, a paralegal who demonstrates insight into the issues to be tried, and the various aspect of pre-trial discovery, will prove the most useful to counsel.

Page 111. Citation Pursuant to SCPA Sec. 1411

Generally, once objections to probate are filed, a decision will be issued directing service of citation pursuant to SCPA Sec. 1411, and setting forth a return date. Forms of citation can be obtained from the court, if need be.

Page 113. (After the Family Tree)

At this juncture, it will be useful to review the section dealing with intestate distribution. Many students will fail to recognize that the laws of intestacy are relevant even in a contested probate proceeding, serving as the basis for determining who must receive citation, and who has standing to object to probate. Similarly, concepts taught in Chapter Three dealing with status are also relevant. For example, a person may claim an interest as a distributee on the basis that he/she is a common law spouse, or an adopted child, or a non-marital child.

Page 115. (After SCPA Sec. 709)

Although the text does not cover, in depth, objections pursuant to SCPA Sec. 709, it should be enhanced through classroom instruction and discussion. Objections to the qualification or eligibility of the named executor can prove useful in avoiding a proceeding for the revocation of letters or removal of the fiduciary once probate is granted.

A person who has standing to object to probate is entitled to object to the granting of letters. Additionally, a legatee who is not a distributee may also file objections, the concept being that such person has an interest in who will be administering the estate. *See Matter of Brumer*, 69 A.D.2d 438 (2d Dept. 1979), *appeal dismissed,* 48 N.Y.2d 667 (1979). Students should be made aware that objections on this ground will not prevent the propounded will from being admitted to probate, assuming it is otherwise a valid instrument. What these objections will accomplish is a stay of the issuance of letters or the appointment of the person against whom the objection is made until the matter is determined.

Students should also be made aware that a party will not be entitled to a jury trial on the issue as to the eligibility of the nominated fiduciary to be appointed. *See Matter of Krom*, 86 A.D.2d 689 (3d Dept. 1982).

Page 115. No Contest Clauses

The subject of no contest clauses can provide for interesting classroom discussion. During the course of discussing this topic, consider asking the class the following questions: what is the rationale for recognizing a no-contest clause? Will a no-contest clause be triggered if a surviving spouse asserts an elective share against an estate? Will a non-contest clause be triggered if objections are made to the qualification or eligibility of the named executor? Will a non-contest clause be triggered if a beneficiary files a claim against the estate to collect a debt? Will a non-contest clause be triggered if an Article 81 guardian files objections to probate on behalf of his ward?

Suggest to the class that a no-contest clause will be most successful in deterring a will contest of the beneficiary(ies) who it is designed to inhibit receive more than a nominal sum under the will. While most beneficiaries will not mind risking a nominal inheritance, an inheritance which is relatively significant in relationship to the value of the estate as a whole will cause a beneficiary to think twice before risking his/her interest if a contest proves unsuccessful.

Page 118. Burden of Proof

At this point in the Chapter, the focus should not only be on the text material, but also on the kinds of pre-trial discovery devices as well as planning devices available to assist in satisfying a party's burden of proof. In terms of planning for a will contest, have students consider the effect of videotaping a will execution ceremony. This will be beneficial provided that the testator appears to be in good physical and mental health, and can, with assuredness, articulate the reasons for the dispositive provisions in his/her will. Additionally, a medical or psychiatric examination of the testator is a good defensive device if the lawyer is confident about the result of the examination and the ability of the physician to serve as a persuasive trial witness. Recall as well that where a contest seems likely, the attesting witnesses to the will should be selected with the thought in mind that they will have to testify at trial. Witnesses who are familiar with the testator will obviously be more persuasive that those who are strangers. Finally, of course, there is the no-contest clause. In terms of discovery devices, introduce the class to such discovery devices as a demand for a bill of particulars, examinations before trial, expert witness demands, and document demands.

Page 119. Testamentary Capacity

Begin the topic of testamentary capacity by informing students that very few wills are denied probate, the rationale being that the law favors the disposition of property by will. Hence, the law looks kindly on wills drawn by the elderly, the frail, and the incapacitated. Thus, while a testator's testamentary capacity must be established, the elements of capacity are pliable and yielding to the circumstances of the testator at the time of the execution of the will. The decision rendered in *In re Estate of Bonafoux* is illustrative of the point. Note the principles upon which the court relied in reaching its decision, i.e., that the decedent had experienced a lucid interval at the time the will was executed. The court also searches for a lucid interval when the claim is made that the testator was suffering from delusions.

In terms of the lawyer's responsibility in supervising the execution of a will of a person who is ill, frail, and possibly delusional, it is his/her responsibility to determine capacity at the time of the execution, through his/her observations of the testator, the testator's responses to questions, the testator's ability to articulate his/her testamentary wishes, and general conversation with the testator regarding such topics as current events, family history, asset information, and such personal matters as age and date of birth.

This discussion will provide a good introduction to those persons whom the law considers to be the best witnesses on the issue of capacity. Have the class consider why a lay witness may be a better witness than an expert witness, why an attesting witness who is familiar with the habits and behavior of the testator is one of the best witnesses, and why an expert witness' testimony may be considered the least reliable. Why is the testimony of an attesting witness given more credence than the testimony of an expert who has reviewed the medical records of the testator? With regard to this question, the decision in *Matter of Van Patten*, 215 A.D.2d 947 (3d Dept. 1995) establishes the prevailing law.

Page 123. Undue Influence

Undue influence is rarely proven through direct evidence. Here, circumstantial evidence is crucial, and must be explored thoroughly in advance of a trial on the issue. With regard to this issue, pre-trial discovery is perhaps the most important for ascertaining proof relevant to those factors expressed by the courts in *Matter of Elmore*, 42 A.D.2d 240 (3d Dept. 1973), and *Matter of Walther*, 6 N.Y.2d 49 (1959).

Page 125. Confidential Relationship

Ask the class why persons having a confidential relationship with the testator are more susceptible to a charge of undue influence than those who are not? Why is it that a family member is not always considered to be in a confidential relationship with a testator? What must be demonstrated before a confidential relationship will be found? Is the law justified in imposing an additional burden on the person who stands in a confidential relationship with the testator to establish that the propounded instrument was voluntarily executed by the testator?

The existence of a confidential relationship between the testator and beneficiary is an important aspect in proving undue influence. Again, detailed exploration of the facts and circumstances surrounding the will should be pursued through examinations before trial of party and non-party witnesses and discovery of documents.

Needless to say, the class should be alerted to the ethical considerations of an attorney drawing a will where he/she is a named beneficiary, even if it is the will of a parent, sibling or other family member, The subject will be explored in greater detail in Chapter Fourteen. Equally disturbing are cases involving spiritual advisors, financial advisors and health care attendants. Have the class consider what facts in those cases were determinative of a confidential relationship between the parties, and a finding of undue influence in the making of the propounded will. The decision in *Matter of Burke*, 82 A.D.2d 260 (2d Dept. 1981) serves as a good instructional tool for this purpose. Ask the class whether it would have affected the outcome in *Burke*, or in any of the other cases discussed in the text for the testator to have expressed either in the will and/or to the attesting witnesses the reasons for the will's dispositive provisions? Should the lawyer, in cases of this nature, and especially where a contest is contemplated, go through the extra precaution of questioning the testator, in front of the attesting witnesses, as to his testamentary wishes, and his/her reasons for favoring a confidant?

Page 127. Fraud

Because fraud is more difficult to establish that undue influence, not much class time should be spent in discussing the subject, except to ensure that the class understands the elements, and that unlike undue influence, fraud must be established by clear and convincing evidence.

Questions to Consider

1. To insure that a testator who cannot speak English duly executes a will, the attorney should make sure that the decedent fully knew and understood the contents of the will. He or she should read the will slowly to the testator, or paraphrase it in terms that the testator can understand. A full translation is not necessary.

2. It is possible that the testator's will can be admitted to probate. The fact that he might have been confused or disoriented within a particular time period does not automatically

require a denial of probate if it can be proved that he executed the will during a lucid interval.

3. The son can make the following arguments for undue influence:

- the will was executed while the testator was in a weakened and disoriented state due to old age and medical ailments
- the provisions were a radical departure from his prior will.
- the daughter had control over her father and his affairs.

The son can make the following arguments for fraud:
- the daughter made willful and false representations that all the son cared about was his father's money.
- she made these statements to deceive her father.
- the statements did deceive her father.
- the false statements caused him to change his will.
- without her interference he would not have changed his will.

4. The son helped choose the law firm, he had connections with law firm about prior business dealings, and he attended the first meeting.

5. The issue of the testator's intent should be raised in the probate proceeding because it is related to the genuineness of the propounded will.

Chapter 7
Revocation of Wills

Chapter Overview

The purpose of this chapter is two-fold: (1) to have students recognize that the revocation of a will requires compliance with statutory formalities; and (2) that many of the statutory formalities required for the revocation of a will are the same as required for the execution of a will. Hence, while wills are ambulatory, and can be revoked by a testator at any time during his/her lifetime, it is important for students to realize that revocation cannot be accomplished to easily. By way of example, ask students whether they think a will can be partially revoked simply by a testator crossing out a paragraph? The answer is "No." Ask students whether they think a will can be revoked in its entirety simply by a testator crossing out three paragraphs? The answer is "No." EPTL Sec. 3-4.1 provides the methods of will revocation, and they are the only methods whereby a will may be revoked. Students should be advised that clients should be discouraged from destroying or attempting a revocation of their will without an attorney's involvement.

Page 133. Capacity

Capacity plays an integral role in the execution and revocation of a will. As in the case of execution of a will, students should realize that a person lacking capacity cannot revoke his/her will. *Matter of Davis,* 154 A.D.2d 461 (2d Dept. 1989) provides an excellent example of the importance of capacity to revocation, and the kind of proof available in order to demonstrate the existence of such capacity. In discussing the case, note the witnesses who were utilized by the proponent of the will to demonstrate revocation of the decedent's prior will- - the decedent's attorney, and health-care professionals who were familiar with his conduct and behavior. In addition, photographs were offered depicting the testator's actions. Point out to the students that this kind of proof is often called upon in contested probate proceedings to demonstrate testamentary capacity.

Page 133. Intention to revoke a will

Students should recognize that a revocation which is unintentional, because it was unknowingly or fraudulently induced or induced by undue influence, is not a valid revocation. For much the same reason as a will procured by undue influence will not be considered valid, so too, a revocation which is unduly influenced will also not be recognized as valid.

While intention is often the subject of direct proof, intention will also be presumed. A case which amply demonstrates this point is *Matter of Bonner*, 17 N.Y2d 9 (1966).

Page 135. (just before dependent relative revocation)

Students should be made aware that the presumption of revocation may be rebutted through circumstantial evidence or direct proof. Ask the students what kind of proof might be sufficient to rebut the presumption? A showing that the attorney last had the original will? A showing that the original will was destroyed by someone other than the testator? A showing that the testator lacked the capacity to revoke his/her will? Oral or written words of the testator pointing to the continued existence of the will? In this latter regard, courts have held that written or oral declarations of the decedent as to the continued existence of the will are inadmissible unless they were made in connection with some act and under such circumstances as to become part of the *res gestae*, i.e. part of the act itself. An example for the class would be where the testator, while shredding business-related documents, shreds his will and immediately thereafter states, " Oh, no. I mistakenly shredded my will." This declaration is admissible as part of the *res gestae.*

Page 135. Dependent Relative Revocation

Recently, the doctrine of dependent relative revocation was applied by the Surrogate's Court, Nassau County, in order to sustain the legatee's status as an objectant to probate. The legatee, who was a beneficiary under a prior, purportedly revoked will of the decedent, argued that any revocation of that prior will was a conditional act, dependent upon the presumed validity of the later, propounded will. Hence, if the propounded will failed, then the prior will could be probated. *In re Estate of Klingele*, N.Y.L.J., Apr. 25, 2002 (Surrogate's Court, Nassau County).

Page 136. Revocation by a writing

Although revocation by a writing may seem easily accomplished, the class should be made aware that non-compliance is the subject of decisions to this day. This only makes clear that when revocation of a will is sought, consultation with an attorney should be sought. Additionally, it should be apparent that an original will should not be left with the testator.

Page 138. Revocation by physical act

This is an aspect of revocation which should prove the subject of interesting class discussion. When is an obliteration, cancellation, or marking on a will a sufficient revocation by physical act? Is burning a whole through the first page of a will sufficient? Is writing "This will is void" across the margin of each page sufficient? Can the physical act of mutilation be one other than described by statute? Is a slight tear in each corner of the will sufficient? Is crossing out three out of ten provisions sufficient? Does it make a difference which provisions are crossed out? What if s copy of the will retained by the testator is torn up, but the original retained by the lawyer remains intact? In discussing these questions, have the class recognize that the revocation by physical act, when accepted as sufficient, go to the essence of the instrument- - either the instrument as a whole, or those portions of the instrument which are significant of its due execution, such as the testator's signature or the signature of the attesting witnesses. Whether a physical act of revocation is sufficient to constitute a revocation is a question of law to be determined by the court and not a jury.

Page 141. Revival and republication of a will

It should be noted that if a will that revokes a prior will is itself revoked and revival does not occur, the testator will die intestate. *Matter of Cleary*, 277 A.D. 893 (2d Dept. 1950). What if the later will does not contain a clause revoking the prior will, will the prior will be revived if the later will is revoked? The answer is "yes". *See Matter of Cunion*, 135 A.D. 864, *affd.*, 201 N.Y. 123 (1909).

Questions to Consider

1. T's act of revocation/alteration is not valid because pursuant to EPTL section 3-4.1(a)(1), a will or any part thereof may be revoked or altered by a writing of the testator clearly indicating an intention to effect such revocation or alteration, executed with the formalities prescribed for the execution or attestation of a will. Because there was no formal execution of this attempted revocation it is not valid.

2. T should include in his new will express language that he is "hereby revoking all prior wills and codicils executed by me".

3. The codicil will revive the will dated May 10, 1997 since it incorporates it by reference. It will also revoke any will dated June 5, 1999, as the codicil is dated July 3, 2000.

4. By destroying the first codicil, the will not affected. Revocation of a codicil to a will does not reinstate the provisions of the will that were changed by the codicil. The second codicil probably revives the 1992 will because incorporates it by reference. The third codicil is valid, but without the terms, it is impossible to know its affect on the will

5. Whether the copy of later will can be admitted to probate depends on whether original was last known to be in possession of T. If so, and can't find original at death, presumption that will was destroyed with intent to revoke. When T's original will can't be found at death and don't know if in his possession, presumption does not arise. Burden on proponent of copy to demonstrate that original not revoked.

Chapter 8
Joint Wills and Mutual Wills

Chapter Overview

Although joint wills are rarely recommended to clients, they have fueled many a court decision, and even provided a basis for legislation. Mutual wills are much more common, particularly where the clients are husband and wife. In fact, many husbands and wives do not even realize that their wills can be categorized as such, and more importantly, can provoke litigation as to whether the instruments constitute a binding contract.

Have the class consider what the benefits of a contractual will might be, especially if they tend to be the subject of litigation. Are they typical in a routine family setting where husband and wife execute wills, or more likely, in a second marriage situation? How might it be possible to ensure that no joint or mutual will will be the subject of litigation as to whether a contract between the parties was intended? Should express words of contract be utilized in all such instruments? Should contractual wills be recognized at all, or should the law require that there always be a separate note or memorandum of contract?

Because the law on contracts finds its way into much of the discussion in this Chapter, a preliminary review of the essential elements of a contract will prove helpful to the class in advance of any instruction with respect to joint and mutual wills.Make sure the class is familiar with the Statute of Frauds and such terms as consideration, meeting of the minds, and intent. In addition, since joint and mutual wills often form the subject of a construction proceeding in the Surrogate's Court, it may prove beneficial to introduce the students to the procedure involved with such a proceeding, and the statute which governs such proceedings in the Surrogate's Court.

Page 145. Joint wills

The class should be informed that the mere execution of a joint will does not create a binding contract between the parties, nor, for that matter, is the execution of a mutual will. The decision in *Matter of Lubins*, 172 Misc.2d 517, *affd*, 250 A.D.2d 850 (2d Dept. 1998) provides an excellent discussion of the subject.

It is important to emphasize to the class that despite the fact that a will is in breach of a contract , it may nevertheless be admitted to probate as a valid testamentary document. *Glass v. Batista*, 43 N.Y.2d 620 (1978). It is equally important for the class to recognize that litigation to enforce the terms of a contract to make a will may be brought in either the Supreme Court or the Surrogate's Court. An example of a Supreme Court action to enforce the terms of a contractual will may be found in the case of *Radici v. Piana*, N.Y.L.J., Mar. 5, 1996 (Supreme Court, New York County). In the Surrogate's Court, the issue may be the subject of a construction proceeding, a miscellaneous proceeding seeking to declare the existence of a contract between the parties, or an accounting proceeding.

What happens however if one of the wills representative of the alleged agreement between the parties is lost? Is the agreement still enforceable? This issue was determined by the Court of Appeals in *Matter of Cohen*, 83 N.Y.2d 148 (1994). The Court held that a contract regarding mutual wills of spouses and outlining their dispositive provisions cannot be enforced if one of the wills is lost when the first spouse dies. The class should be informed that in appropriate cases a lost will may be admitted to probate pursuant to the provisions of SCPA Sec. 1407.

Questions to Consider

1. A's sister does not have a claim for breach of contract by B. There was no evidence that A and B intended to create irrevocable wills and there was no consideration for a contract to make an irrevocable will.

2. B's will is still valid and is admissible to probate. A's niece has a claim against B's estate for breach of the contract between A and B. Possible remedies include damages, turnover of assets to the estate, or the imposition of a constructive trust on the estate assets.

3. C does not have a claim against B's estate because there is no proof that A and B intended to enter into a contract not to amend their wills. Unless it is clear that the parties to joint and mutual wills intend to create irrevocable wills, and the contract is supported by consideration, the court will allow each party to change the will.

4. When the parties have been clear in their intent to enter into irrevocable wills, they cannot make inter vivos gifts that would work to defeat the parties' testamentary plan. One factor courts will examine is whether or not the gifts are substantial. For this reason, A's children and the child born of the marriage of A and B would have a claim for breach of contract. Their claim would be more likely to be sustained if the gifts to B's children were substantial in relation to the size of the estate, so it is more likely that their claim would be sustained if the estate were $2 million rather than $10 million. However, in both cases they would have a strong argument for breach of contract.

Chapter 9
Trusts

Chapter Overview

Students are not apt to understand the concept of a trust as easily as they do the concept of a will. Therefore, the opening pages of Chapter Nine are designed to first introduce students to the terminology associated with trusts and to create a pictorial image of a trust for the class. Indeed, it has become apparent that when a trust is described as a "box" into which property is placed, students are best able to appreciate its meaning and purpose.

Once students understand the concept of a trust and the terminology associated with a trust, the various requirements for creating a trust can be explored in greater detail. The terms income, trust income beneficiary, remainder, and trust remainderman are particularly important for students to understand. Although some students may have become familiar with these terms in their course on property, understanding these terms through examples in class should be reinforced.

Page 156. Elements of a Trust

Before describing the elements of a trust have the class consider some of the reasons why someone would want to utilize a trust as compared to a will for the disposition of his/her property. Bring home to the class that a trust, as compared to a will, can take effect during a grantor's lifetime. Hence, it can prove an effective means of giving property to an individual during life without necessarily giving it outright to that individual. Explain to the class that a trust is an appropriate gift-giving vehicle where there is concern with a particular beneficiary's ability to manage trust property, or where the beneficiary is to receive the gifted property over a period of time, rather than in a lump sum.

Page 158. Intent to create a trust

Impress upon students that intent plays an important role throughout the area of trusts and estates, both in terms of disposing of one's property by will and in gift-giving during one's lifetime. In terms of a trust, the issue of intent rarely arises when the instrument is drafted by an attorney and contains the requisite trust language. However, when a grantor makes a less formal disposition of property, issues may arise as to whether he/she may have intended to make an absolute gift, a trust, an agency relationship, or something else. Under such circumstances, the court may be called upon to determine the grantor's intent.

What type of intent is required to create a trust? What evidence does the court look for in order to determine whether there was a present intent to create a trust? Have the class recognize that the question of intent may be easier in the case of an inter vivos or lifetime trust where the grantor is alive and able to clarify his/her intentions, as compared to a testamentary trust where the grantor is deceased.

Page 159. Trust res

As is evident from the provisions of EPTL Sec. 7-1.5 and EPTL Sec. 3-1.2, with but little exception, every estate in property may be disposed of by lifetime trust. Of interest to the class may be the fact that a seat on the New York Stock Exchange cannot be placed in trust.

Page 160. Eligibility of trustee

The appointment, eligibility, and renunciation of a nominated trustee is not much different than in the case of a named executor under a will. As such, this may be a good time to review both sets of rules and procedural requirements.

One important difference exists in the case where the trustee is also a present income beneficiary of the trust. While this is not a problem in the case where an executor is named as a beneficiary under a will, in the case of a trust, issues may arise where discretionary distributions of income or principal can be made. These issues should be emphasized to the class as they may impact upon the drafting of trust documents and may require an application to the court for the appointment of a co-trustee.

Page 163. Renunciation/resignation of trustee

Point out to eh class that while a trustee can renounce his/her appointment without court approval, a trustee cannot resign without making an application to the court for permission to do so.

Page 165. Interests in trust

Many students will have a difficult time conceptualizing the different interests a beneficiary may have in a trust. However, it is essential for the class to understand these differences in order for them to succeed in the area of trusts and estates administration and litigation. Identifying a beneficiary's interest is necessary in order to properly complete a petition where the affairs of a trust are involved, as may be the case in a probate or accounting proceeding or determine the standing of a party to participate in a proceeding as a litigant. Further, while beyond the scope of this course book, it is necessary to understanding the concept of virtual representation pursuant to the provisions of SCPA Sec. 315.

Page 169. Totten trusts

A totten trust account may b described as an account opened by a person at a financial institution in his own name as trustee for another person. Ordinarily, the depositor retains the right to withdraw the funds at any time during his life, and to have the funds remaining at his death paid to a named beneficiary without subjecting the funds to the probate process. *Caveat:* Totten trust accounts may be subject to the claims of creditors. *See* Chapter 13.

Page 170. Charitable trusts

Charitable trusts are an important section of the chapter on trusts because of their popularity and utility as a tax-savings device. The law favors charitable trusts as is evidenced by the liberal rules of construction invoked by the courts to sustain their validity. Because of the special treatment accorded charitable trusts, in this and many other respects, the law requires that trusts involve some "public benefit" before they will be characterized as charitable. *See generally*, George G. Bogert et. al, Cases and Text on the Law on Trusts, Chapter 10 (7th ed. 2001). Ask the class for some examples of trusts which may be considered "charitable" because they benefit the public good.

Page 172. Constructive trusts

The class should be informed that as compared to an express trust, a constructive trust is not a legal relationship based on the intent of the parties. It is a fraud-rectifying rather than an intent-enforcing trust.

Point out to the class that the decree adjudging that a constructive trust exists will order the constructive trustee to convey title to the disputed property to the beneficiary. Probably one of the most of-cited cases on the subject of constructive trusts is *Sharp v. Kosmalski*, 40 N.Y.2d 119 (1976).

Page 174. Amendment and termination of trusts

On the subject of a trust amendment and termination, ask the class why a grantor would not always reserve in himself or herself the power to amend or revoke a trust. In the absence of such reserved right, the grantor will be required to obtain the consent of the trust beneficiaries to an amendment or revocation. This may sometimes be the cause of controversy between the parties. On the other hand, adverse tax consequences may result where a grantor reserves a right to amend or revoke the trust.

Questions to Consider

1. a. A transfer of "most of my property" is not a valid trust transfer because it is not sufficiently identifiable.
b. A life estate can be transferred in trust.
c. "literary property" can be transferred in trust so long as the property transferred is clearly identified.

d. "an expectant recovery in a lawsuit" can be transferred in trust so long as the lawsuit is clearly identified. The beneficiaries would have a contingent future interest because they would only benefit if the lawsuit was successful.

2. Yes, this transfer is valid. Although the will itself needs two witnesses to be valid, a trust can be created either orally or in writing. The letter signed by the testator would be sufficient to create a trust.

3. A is not entitled to the proceeds of the totten trust account. The EPTL specifically provides that a totten trust may be terminated in the depositor's will.

4. a. A trust created during the lifetime of the grantor is an inter vivos trust.
b. A trust where the trustee has no active duties of management is a passive trust.
c. A trust created by operation of law in order to prevent fraud is a constructive trust.
d. A trust that is usually in the form of a savings bank account is a totten trust.
e. A trust designed to protect the interest of a beneficiary from creditors is a spendthrift trust.

5. If C dies during the term of the trust, it will be necessary for the court to appoint a successor trustee because with C's death, A became the sole trustee and the sole beneficiary, which will cause the legal and beneficial interests to merge and will terminate the trust.

6. The charitable trust will not be invalid. The court will likely invoke the cy pres doctrine to save the trust, because charitable trusts are favored by the law. This doctrine allows the court to revise the bequest in a way that would fulfill the decedent's charitable intent. In this case, the training of Collie puppies is sufficiently similar to the training of German Shepherd puppies.

7. The Grantor may not terminate the trust because it was irrevocable, so the Grantor has no rights to the trust or to the trust property.

8. The decedent has created a passive trust, which is not valid in New York, so that 10% of the decedent's estate would probably be given to the two grandchildren outright, in equal parts.

Chapter 10
Gifts

Chapter Overview

The concepts in the Chapter on gifts should prove the least difficult for students to understand. Indeed, gifts are tangible; gifts are part of everyday living. The elements of a gift are straightforward: donative intent, delivery and acceptance. Donative intent should be emphasized as a concept that runs throughout trusts and estates practice finding itself in the making and revocation of a will, as well as the creation of a trust. Note that donative intent is very much interwoven with the concept of capacity.

Page 180. Donative intent

Perhaps the most significant cases regarding the element of donative intent, and the concept of gifts as a whole are *Matter of Szabo*, 10 N.Y.2d 94 (1961), *Gruen v. Gruen*, 68 N.Y.2d 48 (1986), and *Speelman v. Pascal*, 10 N.Y.2d 313 (1961).

With regard to the issue of capacity to make a gift point out to the class the similarity between the court's analysis, where the validity of a gift is at issue and where the validity of a will is at issue. In both situations, the recipient of either the lifetime gift or testamentary gift is required to demonstrate that the transaction was fair and voluntary. The decision in *Spallina v. Giannoccaro*, 98 A.D.2d 103 (4th Dept. 1983) sets forth the prevailing law in this regard.

The element of acceptance speaks for itself, and is presumed when something of value or which is beneficial to the recipient is being given away.

Page 184. Delivery

The element of delivery may be the only element which may prove a bit confusing to the class inasmuch as the delivery of a gift item may take many forms-actual, constructive, or symbolic. What must be emphasized is the donor must give up dominion and control of the object or item which is the subject of the gift for delivery to be effective and complete.

The more examples which can be given to the class by way of cases in the text or otherwise, the more useful it will to conveying the concept of delivery within the gift-giving context. Again, the decisions in *Matter of Szabo, supra.* and *Matter of Gruen, supra.* provide a good recitation of the law in regard to this issue.

Another interesting decision on the subject was rendered in *In re Estate of Kondo*, N.Y.L.J., Dec. 5, 2001 (Surrogate's Court, New York County). This was a turnover proceeding against the fiduciary by a claimant who alleged that the decedent's family was withholding certain jewelry which the decedent had given him as a gift before death. As evidence of the gift, the claimant offered a letter written by the decedent which was

translated, in pertinent part, to read: "I will give jewels in safety deposit box to Harry..."
or "I am giving jewelry in the safe to Harry..."

With respect to the element of intent, the court found that the words "I am giving"
or "I will I've" were not indicative of a present donative intent. Further, the court found
insufficient delivery of the gift. The court noted that the property in question remained in
the decedent's safe in her co-op until she died. The court held:

> There is ample case law to the effect that an alleged donor's continued
> possession of property until her death is generally inconsistent with a
> claim of completed delivery of the purported gift. This is so even where
> the alleged donee has been given joint custody...since delivery normally
> cannot occur unless the deceased alleged donor has divested himself of all
> control over the subject property.

Note: In support of its holding, the court cited the decision in *Matter of Kennedy's Estate*,
56 Misc.2d 1092 (1964), which appears at page **179** of the text.

Questions to Consider

1. In this fact situation it is doubtful that constructive delivery occurred. Constructive
delivery can be accomplished by a written instrument, but the written instrument must
expressly state that a present gift is intended, not one to be given in the future. In the
present case the decedent's letter to Harold stated that he would like Harold to oversee
his estate and disposal of his assets "in the event that I should pass away or become
incapacitated mentally". This letter indicates that the transfer was to occur in the future.
Second, constructive delivery may also occur by the transfer of keys to a safe deposit
box, but only if circumstances do not permit actual delivery of the contents of the box
and the donor relinquishes all dominion and control over the contents of the box. Again,
in his letter to Harold, the decedent says that he "would deliver" the keys to Harold, but
there is no evidence that that delivery ever occurred or that the decedent gave up any
dominion or control over the contents of the box.

2. The deed constitutes a valid inter vivos gift, as all of the requirements were met. The
decedent was alert and oriented and executed the deed with free will, showing donative
intent. The deed was obviously delivered and accepted, since it was later recorded. The
decedent's receipt of income pursuant to the deed does not mean that he did not intend an
irrevocable transfer of the fee interest.

3. The decedent's delivery of the automobile keys constituted both a valid inter vivos gift
and a valid gift causa mortis. In handing his brother in law the keys, he said "take it, it's
yours", clearly indicating present intent to make a gift. Because of his ill health he was
unable to locate and sign the title, so that delivery of the keys constituted effective
constructive delivery. The gift was also a gift causa mortis because at the time of the gift,
the decedent knew that he was going to die from his illness and a week later he did in fact
die from that illness.

4. The burden of proof is on the son to show a valid gift and in this situation it is doubtful that he met this burden. The letter was prepared entirely by the son, and at the time that his father signed it he was sick and dying. The letter also never clearly stated that the father intended to give his artwork to his son. Finally, the facts that the father never told his wife about the gift and that the son told the wife that he was only going to catalogue the artwork also suggest that no gift was intended.

Chapter 11
Jurisdiction and Power of the Surrogate's Court

Chapter Overview

The chapter of jurisdiction discusses the rudiments of Surrogate's Court practice, subject matter jurisdiction and personal jurisdiction. In teaching subject matter jurisdiction, the following should be emphasized: (1) that subject matter jurisdiction cannot be waived; (2) that the subject matter jurisdiction of the Surrogate's Court is with respect to all matters relating to the affairs of a decedent and the administration of a decedent's estate; and (3) that the Surrogate's Court lacks subject matter jurisdiction over independent controversies between living persons.

Page 194. The provisions of SCPA 202

The Surrogate's Court's jurisdiction is broadly based and is often exercised with respect to matters that most students would typically associate with the jurisdiction of the Supreme Court. Point out to the students that this broad base of authority is largely the result of the New York State Constitution's grant of authority to the Surrogate's Court as well as the provisions of SCPA Sec. 202 which authorizes the Surrogate's Court to hear and determine a matter over which it has subject matter jurisdiction despite the absence of a specific statute in the SCPA authorizing the proceeding or the kind of relief being sought.

Pages 195. *Piccione* and *Lainez*

While *Matter of Piccione* and *Matter of Lainez* are the best known cases on the question of subject matter jurisdiction, additional cases which are instructive appear in the text at page **189**.

Page 197. Jurisdiction over estates of domiciliary decedents

Once it is determined that the Constitutional mandates of subject matter jurisdiction exist, the question becomes whether the subject of the proceeding has a sufficient nexus to this State for subject matter jurisdiction to be exercised. In other words, although a proceeding may relate to the affairs of a decedent or the administration of an estate, if it does not have a relationship to New York State, the Surrogate's Court will decline jurisdiction. The necessary connection or relationship to the State is defined by the provisions of SCPA Secs. 205, 206, and 207. It is recommended that these statutory sections be examined within this context, so that the class is clear as to the nature and extent of the statutory requirements and the kind of nexus needed before subject matter jurisdiction will be had.

Page 199. Matter of Obregon

While there are few decisions of interest under SCPA Sec. 205 and SCPA Sec. 206, the decision by the Court of Appeals in *Matter of Obregon,* 91 N.Y.2d 591 (1998) received much attention when it was rendered.

Page 199. Matter of Petras

The decision in *Matter of Petras*, N.Y.L.J., Jun. 9, 1995 (Surrogate's Court, New York County), is also provided as a useful tool for exploring the factors considered by the court in determining whether to exercise its discretion and assume jurisdiction over the estate of a non-domiciliary. Again, it should be noted that the sufficiency of New York contacts is the primary consideration.

Page 201. Personal Jurisdiction

In discussing the Surrogate's Court's personal jurisdiction over the parties to a proceeding, keep in mind that issues relative to long arm jurisdiction are rarely encountered. Emphasis should therefore be placed upon the provisions of SCPA Sec. 307 and SCPA Sec. 401, governing of citation and the appearance of a party. Indeed, the class should be forewarned that in most law offices the responsibility for insuring that personal jurisdiction is obtained over the necessary parties rests with the paralegal.

Page 203. Appearance for an infant

An understanding of when and under what circumstances a guardian ad litem is appointed is also essential. The class should be aware that a guardian ad litem is frequently appointed by the Surrogate's Court to represent persons under a disability and that in most instances it will be the paralegal to interface with him/her regarding the proceeding and its status.

Page 205. Service of process

The discussion in the text regarding the provisions of SCPA Secs. 307-309 is straightforward and should be examined with the class in the manner presented, utilizing as many examples as possible to ensure understanding .

Page 207. Power of the court

On a final note is the concept of the Surrogate's Court's power, as defined by the provisions of SCPA Sec. 209. The need for the paralegal(as compared to the attorney) to resort to this statute will be rare, and thus, while it should be mentioned and discussed, it is given brief treatment in the text.

Questions to Consider

1. a. The Surrogate's Court would not have jurisdiction over an action between the beneficiary of an estate and his attorney because this is an action between two living persons.

b. The Surrogate's Court would have jurisdiction over a claim based upon a breach of a separation agreement between the decedent and his surviving spouse because this claim affects the estate.

c. The Surrogate's Court would have jurisdiction over a claim based upon unpaid royalties due the decedent's estate because this affects the estate and it is a claim for moneys belonging to the estate.

d. The Surrogate's Court would not have jurisdiction over a claim for medical malpractice committed by a non-domiciliary physician against a New York decedent unless the malpractice occurred in New York. If the malpractice occurred outside of New York, then New York courts would not have personal jurisdiction over the physician, and this would properly be brought as an ancillary administration claim in the state where the physician was domiciled.

e. The Surrogate's Court has jurisdiction over guardianship proceedings.

f. The Surrogate's Court would not have jurisdiction over a claim by a creditor against an estate beneficiary for an unpaid debt because this is a claim between two living persons.

g. The Surrogate's Court would have jurisdiction over a suit for eviction against a holdover tenant in property that is an asset of the estate because the outcome of the suit affects the value of the estate.

2. The following facts are relevant to the consideration of whether the Surrogate's Court in Suffolk County should assume jurisdiction: the decedent died domiciled in CT, the trust corpus is in CT, and both trustees of the trust are located in CT.

3. The decedent's adult children may not appear for the decedent's infant grandchild. However, if one of the adult children is the guardian of the property of the infant grandchild, then that person may appear so long as he or she complies with the statutory requirements of SCPA Section 402(1).

4. If the return date of the citation is August 21, 2001, then service must be made as follows:
a. adult son residing in New York: August 21.
b. spouse residing in New York: August 21.
c. infant nephew residing in New Jersey with his mother: August 11.
d. infant grandchild residing with his mother in New York: August 21.

5. a. & b. Service should be made by personal delivery or by registered or certified mail, return receipt requested. If these methods are not possible service may be made by court order. Proof is made to the court in the same manner set forth in CPLR sections 306 and 4532.

c. Service on an infant in New Jersey should be made by registered or certified mail, return receipt requested, or by special mail service, in all cases upon his mother. However, if the infant is 14 years old or older, service may be made on him personally. Proof of service is the same as above, except that if the infant is under 16, he cannot admit service in writing.

d. Service on an infant grandchild in New York should be made by registered or certified mail, return receipt requested, upon his mother on his behalf. However, if the infant is 14 years old or older, service may be made on him personally. Proof of service is the same as above, except that if the infant is under 16, he cannot admit service in writing.

Chapter 12
Venue

Chapter Overview

Chapter Twelve presents a discussion of venue, a subject which, like jurisdiction, is based upon the contacts between the subject matter of a proceeding and the county in which it is brought. This is often based upon the location or situs of assets, as in the case of non-domiciliary decedents and lifetime trusts, or in the case of domiciliary decedents, the county of the decedent's domicile at death.

Page 212. Domiciliary decedents

The question of venue in the context of domiciliary decedents is most often encountered in the Surrogate's Court, and, as compared to other questions of venue, is most often litigated. Hence, it is recommended time be spent on this portion of the chapter, with particular emphasis on those factors which are considered relevant in the determination of domicile. The decisions in *Matter of Urdang*, 194 A.D.2d 615 (2d Dept. 1993) and *Matter of Newcomb*, 192 N.Y. 238 (1908) are often cited in respect to this issue. Furthermore, the New York State Department of Taxation and Finance established its own set of considerations and factors to be invoked in assessing domicile, for purposes of New York State income taxation. These appear in the District Office Audit Manual, found in CCH, New York Tax Reports, Par.19-600, pp. 8206 et. seq. (1998). Because the Audit Manual provides a comprehensive study and approach to the subject of domicile, it may prove worthwhile to share its contents with the class.

Page 217. Transfer of venue

With regard to the transfer of venue, the decisions in *Matter of Dickinson*, 129 Misc.2d 184 (1985) and *In re Estate of Dickinson*, N.Y.L.J., Nov. 24, 1998 (Surrogate's Court, Nassau County) are instructive.

Questions to Consider

1. Given that the decedent resided in Dutchess County for over three years, he probably died domiciled in Dutchess County. The court would review various factors relevant to his intent, including the location of his assets, his mailing address, the residence listed on his driver's license, if he had one, where he was registered to vote and how often he voted at that location, the residence addresses of his friends and family, where any business was located at the time of his death, his place of worship, if any, where he had any memberships in local clubs or organizations, and the location of his safe deposit box, if any.

2. Both Nassau County and Kings County had venue over this matter, because one of the trustees of the trust resided in Nassau County and a portion of the trust assets were

located in Kings County. When more than one county has venue, the first county where proceedings are commenced retains venue. Therefore, the proceedings the Kings County should be transferred to Nassau County and all of the matters resolved in one proceeding in Nassau County.

3. The proper venue would be the decedent's domicile at the time of his death. Domicile is a person's fixed, permanent home, to which he intends to return, so the key question is the person's intent. In this situation, assuming that the decedent still owned the home in Queens County at the time of his death, he was probably still domiciled in Queens County and that would be the proper venue for proceedings related to his estate. At the time that the decedent was removed from his home to the various homes and care facilities in Suffolk County, he was confused and disoriented and likely did not have the capacity to intend to change his domicile from Queens County to Suffolk County.

4. According to SCPA Section 206, Broome County would be the proper venue because it is where property belonging to the non-domiciliary decedent has, since his death, come into and remains unadministered. If a fiduciary had already been appointed in Pennsylvania, the Broome County Surrogate's Court would probably defer to Pennsylvania courts for the administration of the estate because the decedent was domiciled in Pennsylvania and Pennsylvania had a much greater connection to the decedent.

Chapter 13
Fiduciary Duties in Administering an Estate.

Chapter Overview

For the paralegal who concentrates in the field of trusts and estates, estate administration will most likely prove to be the focal point of his/her job responsibilities. Even those paralegals who sub-specialize in estate litigation should have a working knowledge of this area. Therefore, it is essential that this chapter of the book be examined methodically with the class, and that steps are taken to ensure a full understanding of the topics covered.

Page 222. Pre-Probate

Most paralegals and most lawyers, for that matter, are unaware of the pre-probate responsibilities of the named executor in a will as evidenced by the decision in *Matter of Donner*, 82 N.Y.2d 574 (1993) this can result in unanticipated substantial liability to a nominated fiduciary. In reviewing the facts of the case, have the class consider the pre-death relationship between the nominated fiduciaries and the decedent and the particular awareness they had of her assets and affairs. Ask the class whether the special knowledge of the fiduciaries precipitated the result. In other words, if the nominated fiduciaries in the *Donner* case did not have as much access to information regarding the decedent's securities and their volatility, would they have been held liable?

Additionally, the *Donner* case is significant with respect to the issue of the joint and several liability of estate fiduciaries. Note that one of the fiduciaries in *Donner* did not have personal experience with the decedent's portfolio but was held accountable due to the actions of his co-fiduciaries. This theory was also applied in *Matter of Rothko,* 84 Misc.2d 830, *modified*, 56 A.D.2d 499, 43 N.Y.2d 305 (1977) perhaps one of the most well known cases in the field dealing with issues related to self-dealing, conflict of interest , and joint and several liability of fiduciaries, as well as *Matter of Yarm*, 119 A.D.2d 754 (2d Dept. 1986)

Page 223. Duties of the Appointed Fiduciary

It is important for the class to realize that while the theoretical responsibility for administering an estate rests with the fiduciary, in practice, the responsibility falls upon counsel for the estate. Hence, the class should approach this portion of the chapter with the understanding that it is they who will be fulfilling most of the duties described. The class should understand that an attorney cannot be compensated for performing executorial services. Hence, to the extent that the fees of counsel for the estate become an issue, the sum requested will be reduced by the amount charged for executorial work.

Page 225. Opening an estate account

It is often time the notion of a surviving heir, especially a surviving spouse, who is serving as a fiduciary, that they may combine estate assets with their own, the thought being that most, if not all, the estate property will be going to him/her anyway. The fiduciary should be cautioned from the outset that this is impermissible. The optimum means of preventing this, of course, is for counsel to administer the estate accounts, making deposits and withdrawals over the fiduciary's signature, as and when needed.

Page 226. Collecting assets

Note that while the typical methods of collecting an asset are set forth, the paralegal should attempt to contact the institution housing the asset in order to determine whether it requires something additional.

Page 228. Appraisal

The appraisal and valuation process may take longer than anticipated, especially where the valuation of a business is concerned. Hence, the appraisal process should begin from the inception of the estate administration. Point out to the class, however, that some assets will have to be appraised as of the date of death as well as six months from death, i.e. the alternate valuation date, in order to determine the value which will achieve the most estate tax benefits.

Page 231. Fiduciary may not pay personal claim

As in the case where a surviving heir/fiduciary may think it non-problematic to commingle estate and personal funds, so too, a surviving heir/fiduciary may believe it is not a problem to satisfy his/her personal claim against the estate. The fiduciary should be cautioned against engaging in such conduct, except in accordance with the provisions of SCPA Sec. 1805.

Page 231. Administration expenses

Expenses incurred by the fiduciary in the course of administering an estate are always subject to scrutiny, either by the court or the estate beneficiaries. The fiduciary should be cautioned that in retaining a third party to perform work on behalf of the estate, he/she should always sign the contract in a fiduciary capacity, and not individually. The effect of this is to limit the third party recovery for services rendered to estate assets, and not individual assets of the estate fiduciary.

Page 233. Abatement

The abatement statute provides a valuable lesson to the class to the extent of demonstrating that a testamentary plan can sometimes be sacrificed to creditors' claims. Have the class consider how and to what extent proper estate planning might help avoid the impact of the statute. The class should understand that proper estate planning requires that the attorney obtain information not only with regard to the testator's assets, but also with regard to his/her liabilities.

Page 233. Byfield case

The decision in *In re Estate of Byfield*, N.Y.L.J., Oct. 30, 1996 (Surrogate's Court, Westchester County) provides a good synopsis regarding the law on abatement, particularly as it applies to non-testamentary property.

Page 234. Payment of taxes

The failure to timely file a tax return and pay taxes due, which is attributable to the oversight of counsel for the estate, can result in the liability of the estate fiduciary, and concomitantly, his/her attorney. Because of the multiple tax filings with which the paralegal may be involved, students should be advised to prepare a calendar of important dates at the inception of each estate, and to refer to that calendar on a daily basis.

Page 234. Income in respect of decedent

The concept of income in respect of a decedent is often difficult to understand. It is important that the class grasp the theory inasmuch as it plays an integral role in the income and estate taxation of an estate.

Page 235. Federal/New York Tax

Although the course book introduces students to the concept of estate tax filings and preparation, the best learning device in this regard is the actual preparation of a return. To the extent there is time, a practical exercise requiring the preparation of an estate tax return would be worthwhile. Note that while much of the computation is now done by computer, proper input is the responsibility of the paralegal. An understanding of the line items and schedules of the return can thus be ensured through this suggested practical approach.

Page 244. Demand for payment

In order to appreciate the contrary views as to whether a demand for payment is necessary, the decisions in *Matter of LaFave*, 116 Misc.2d 918 (1982) and *Matter of Schwarz*, 161 Misc.2d 471 (1994) can be helpful.

Page 246. Duty to account

An essential function of the fiduciary is his/her duty to account to the estate beneficiaries. To this extent, proper maintenance of books and records is essential. A fiduciary's failure to maintain proper books and records will result in an incomplete and/or inaccurate accounting, and more often than not, litigation regarding the fiduciary's stewardship. The class should be informed that in more cases than not, the responsibility for maintaining the estate books and records as well as for preparing an accounting will fall upon the paralegal students should be made to realize that a receipt and release based upon an improper or incomplete accounting will not be binding. When litigation is commenced, well maintained books and records are invaluable to the fiduciary who must defend his /her stewardship. Receipts and invoices will likely have to be produced, as will transaction statements regarding sales, appraisals, checkbooks, and correspondence between the fiduciary and the beneficiaries and counsel. The class should recognize that not all communications between the fiduciary and estate counsel are privileged, and that the privilege only attaches once litigation has commenced or is anticipated.

Page 252. Advance payment

A common trap for the unwary fiduciary is to pay himself/herself advance commissions without court approval. The fiduciary, particularly one with control over the estate checkbook should be cautioned that an advance payment without such approval may result in his/her approval being surcharged at the rate of 9% per annum.

Page 253. Legal Fees

The decisions in *Matter of Freeman*, 34 N.Y.2d 1 (1974) and *Matter of Potts*, 213 A.D. 59, *affd.*, 241 N.Y. 593 (1925) are perhaps two of the most oft-cited decisions addressing legal fees. Because the estate paralegal will generally prepare at least an initial draft of an affidavit of legal services on behalf of counsel, the paralegal's understanding of the criteria established by these cases, as well as by the provisions of UCR 207.45, is essential.

Questions to Consider

1. a. Pursuant to the provisions of SCPA Section 2120(4) and EPTL Section 11-1.5, a proceeding may be commenced against the fiduciary to pay a legacy or distributive share of an estate after the expiration of seven months from the issuance of permanent letters.

b. The son is only entitled to interest once the legacy is late, so he would be entitled to interest beginning seven months after the issuance of letters, at the rate of 6% per annum.

c. The son is not entitled to income because his is a general legacy.

2. The executor should make certain that the house remains in good repair and is insured, and that the works of art are safe and insured. He may also sell the stock and reinvest the proceeds to make certain that it continues to be income producing.

3. The order of the debt payments would be:
   - first: $75,000 administration and funeral expenses, with the administration expenses coming before the funeral expenses;
   - second: $50,000 outstanding taxes;
   - third: $400,000 secured debts; and
   - fourth: $100,000 general creditors.

The total debts are $625,000, and the estate is valued at $550,000, leaving a shortfall of $75,000. Since there is $300,000 in the residuary estate, the entire deficit will abate from the residuary.

4. A should pursue an informal accounting under SCPA Section 2203, which allow the fiduciary to be discharged without a formal accounting.

5. Executor's commissions would be as follows:

a. commissions on receiving:

cash	$ 250,000
securities	1,500,000
refund	2,500
jewelry	70,000
income	15,000
TOTAL	$1,837,500

2.5% x 100,000 =	$ 2,500.00
2% x 200,000 =	4,000.00
1.5% x 700,000 =	10,500.00
1.25% x 837,500 =	10,468.75
TOTAL =	$27,468.75

b. commissions on paying:

expenses	$ 40,000
claims	10,000
distributions	60,000
balance on hand	1,712,500
TOTAL	$1,822,500

2.5% x 100,000 =	$ 2,500.00
2% x 200,000 =	4,000.00
1.5% x 700,000 =	10,500.00
1.25% x 712,500 =	8,906.25
TOTAL =	$25,906.25

$25,906.25
+ 27,468.75
$53,375.00 = Commissions on estate.

6. The legal criteria for fixing legal fees are the size of the estate, the difficulties involved, the nature of the legal services rendered, the time spent, the professional standing of the counsel and the results obtained. The affidavit should state when and by whom the attorney was retained, the terms of the retainer, the amount of compensation requested, whether the client has been consulted as to the fee requested, whether the

client consents to the fee of if not, the nature of the disagreement, the period during which services were rendered, the services rendered, the time spent, the method for determining the fee requested, whether the fee includes all services rendered, and whether the attorney waives a formal hearing as to compensation.

7. Secure estate assets

Institute proceedings for probate or administration
Marshal estate assets
Pay debts and expenses
Satisfy legacies (Sept. 2000)
File estate tax and pay estate taxes (Nov. 22, 2000)
File the decedent's final income tax return (April 15, 2001)
Account to the beneficiaries

8. The steps required to marshal a decedent's bank accounts and registered securities are:

a. Bank Accounts
- the fiduciary should write a letter of instruction, with signature guaranteed;
- the fiduciary should present the passbook for a savings account or the certificate in the case of a certificate of deposit;
- the fiduciary should sign a withdrawal form or slip, with signature guaranteed by a commercial bank officer or stock broker; and
- the fiduciary should present a short form certificate of letters testamentary or letters of administration, dated within 60 days of the withdrawal.

b. Registered Securities
- the fiduciary should write a letter of instruction, with signature guaranteed;
- the fiduciary should present the stock certificates in the decedent's name, or, if lost, an affidavit and indemnity agreement;
- the fiduciary should present a signed stock power, with signature guaranteed by a commercial bank officer or stock broker;
- the fiduciary should present an affidavit of decedent's domicile;
- the fiduciary should present a short form certificate of letters testamentary or letters of administration, dated within 60 days of the collection; and
- the fiduciary should present a W-9 form.

Chapter 14
Ethical Issues Confronting the Paralegal

Chapter Overview

While ethical considerations are of vital importance to the practice of law, in the classroom setting they seem to play an incidental role. Perhaps because of the methodology by which codes and canons of ethics are taught, perhaps because students do not realize they will routinely affect their job responsibilities, perhaps because they do not oversee themselves confronted with an ethical dilemma on a professional level, students take very little interest in learning this subject. In order to overcome this potential laissez-faire sentiment, a recommended approach to teaching this chapter may be through use of role playing. This form of pedagogy has proven a useful instructional device in many classroom situations and should serve to generate student interest and participation.

If role playing would not be appropriate for the class, consider as an alternative, posing to students various hypothetical situations with an ethical component which they must address. For example, place the student in a situation where he/she is requested by a lawyer in the firm to perform a task which could be categorized as the unauthorized practice of law. Ask the students how they would respond if confronted with such a request. Or, have the students consider how they would, if at all, approach a situation where the lawyer with whom they work, is drafting a will making him or her the recipient of a bequest, or the named executor. Does the paralegal have a responsibility to discuss the ethical concerns of this situation with the lawyer? The client? Should a paralegal draft a will or participate in a will execution where the lawyer is a named beneficiary?

Separate and apart from role playing and hypotheticals, the chapter on ethical responsibility can best be taught by selecting key topics on the subject and making them the focus of class instruction and discussion. No student should be required or expected to memorize ethical codes but a student should be made sensitive to issues which may present an ethical consideration, and should be made well aware of the kind of conduct which may result in disciplinary action.

Page 266. Unauthorized practice of law

One of the more essential components of the chapter which should certainly be the subject of classroom discussion is the unauthorized practice of law. It is important for paralegals to know and understand the boundary which divides those services which they are authorized to perform and those which constitute the unauthorized practice of law. Crossing the dividing line could subject the paralegal and the attorney for whom he/she works to possible disciplinary action. The text provides various examples of what constitutes the unauthorized practice of law, as well as ethical codes and standards established by the American Bar Association, the New York Code of Professional Responsibility, and the National Association of Legal Assistants. The significance of this area should be taken seriously by the students, and should be emphasized and re-emphasized through examples to the students.

Page 272. Attorney-client privilege

A second essential topic covered in Chapter Fourteen is the attorney-client privilege. Understanding the scope of the attorney-client privilege from an evidentiary as well as an ethical perspective will guide the paralegal not only with respect to his/her own ethical responsibilities, but also with regard to the conduct of litigation and document production. Indeed, for the paralegal who assists in litigation, knowing what material is privileged and what material constitutes attorney work- product or material prepared in anticipation of litigation is essential. Lawyers rarely have the time to sift through material which is called for in a document demand. Hence, the burden falls upon the paralegal to determine or at the very least be sensitive to those items which should be withheld on the basis of privilege.

Page 274. Attorney draftsman of a will

The third and final topic which should be emphasized in class coverage of chapter 14 is the ethical rules and responsibilities governing the attorney-draftsman of a will. The decisions in *Matter of Weinstock*, 40 N.Y.2d 1 (1976) and *Matter of Putnam*, 257 N.Y. 140 (1931) are of paramount importance to trusts and estates practitioners as they should be to the trusts and estates paralegal. In discussing each of these cases, note the following: (1) that these cases deal with ethical restraints on the attorney-draftsman only; (2) that the ethical concerns for full disclosure and fair dealing which both opinions impart can be cured either: (a) by having independent counsel draft the document, or (b) by having the client sign an affidavit indicating the circumstances surrounding the disposition or benefit conferred upon the attorney (*see e.g.* SCPA 2307-a); (3) the probate petition serves as a means for the court to monitor wills naming an attorney as beneficiary and/or as executor; and (4) UCR 207.52 serves as a means of overseeing the legal fees charged by an attorney-fiduciary.

Questions to Consider

1. Ethical canons are general concepts of acceptable and ethical behavior, while disciplinary rules are specific and mandatory rules which state the minimum level of conduct below which no lawyer can fall without being subject to disciplinary action.

2. When performed by a paralegal,

> a. Interviewing prospective trial witnesses does not constitute the unlawful practice of law.
> b. supervising the execution of a contract of sale does not constitute the unlawful practice of law, as long as the paralegal is supervised and does not make legal judgments.

c. closing on a parcel of real estate does constitute the unlawful practice of law; the paralegal may assist in the closing, but the attorney should conduct the closing.

d. a paralegal may attend a court conference with a supervising attorney, but not alone.

e. a paralegal may take notes during a deposition conducted by the lawyer.

f. a paralegal may not discuss a possible fee arrangement with a potential client.

g. a paralegal may not render an opinion as to whether a matter can be settled.

h. a paralegal may not provide information as to when opposition papers to a motion must be filed unless the client is aware that he or she is talking to a paralegal and the paralegal has obtained this information directly from the lawyer and has been instructed by the lawyer to pass it along to the client.

3. a. A communication among the attorney and client and the client's spouse would be protected because the spouse is not a stranger. However, in a proceeding between the husband and wife, the two would be adversaries and this communication would not be protected.

b. A communication among the attorney and client in the presence of a legal assistant would be privileged if the legal assistant is a subordinate of the lawyer and is involved in the matter relating to the communication.

c. A communication between a client and attorney regarding the financial outlook for the coming year would not be privileged unless it related to a matter in which the attorney was representing the client.

4. Although generally the power to waive the attorney client privilege terminates with the death of the client, the privilege could be waived (i) if the validity of the gift related to the probate, validity or construction of his or her will, (ii) could be waived by the personal representative of the estate, or (iii) could be waived by an objectant in a probate proceeding if it is in the best interest of the estate.

5. a. Witness interviews may be considered as attorney work product or as materials prepared in anticipation of litigation, depending on their nature. If conducted by an attorney they would be considered as attorney work product. They could also be materials prepared in anticipation of litigation if prepared by a client at the request of the attorney.

b. An attorney's memorandum regarding case strategy is protected as attorney client work product.

c. Notes or revisions made by a client on a contract sent to the attorney may be protected under the attorney-client privilege, but it is not attorney work product or material prepared in anticipation of litigation.

d. Client notes regarding the occurrence of an accident constitutes material prepared in anticipation of litigation.

e. Witness statements obtained by an attorney constitutes material prepared in anticipation of litigation.

7. The problem in this case is that the attorney will also be a material witness in the matter. The disciplinary rules require that an attorney who knows that he will be called as

a witness on behalf of the client should not accept employment, or should withdraw once he knows about the conflict. The courts will, however, usually allow the attorney to represent his client in all pretrial stages, so in this fact situation the attorney could represent the client in pretrial discovery.

Chapter 15
Resources for the Practicing Paralegal

The purpose of Chapter Fifteen is to ensure the on-going professional and intellectual enhancement of the paralegal by providing students with resources which can be referred to in their career. Students should be told that their paralegal education is but one ste of the way towards a successful career. Continuing education courses, keeping current with respect to legal developments in their area of concentration and knowing where to find the answers when a problem is presented will lead to greater professional skills and recognition at the workplace.

TEST BANK

Chapter 2
The Laws of Intestacy

A. Multiple Choice

1. Mr. Edwards died with a will but the will made no mention of his hunting cottage, nor did it contain a residuary clause. What will happen to the hunting cottage?
a. it will belong to the State of New York.
b. it will go to his cousin Bob because he used it.
c. it will pass by the laws of intestacy in New York.
d. it will belong to the first person who claims it.

2. Molly is related to her first cousin by how many degrees of consanguinity?
a. 2.
b. 3.
c. 4.
d. 5

3. Which of the following is Tim's lineal ancestor?
a. his first cousin.
b. his great great grandfather.
c. his sister.
d. his uncle.

4. When a person dies intestate, the fiduciary who will handle his or her estate is called
a. an administrator
b. an executor
c. an intestate manager
4. a distributee

5. A person's fixed, permanent and principal home, to which he or she intends to return when away is that person's
a. residence
b. homestead
c. domicile
d. family estate.

6. Sarah's granddaughter is her
a. lineal ancestor
b. lineal descendant
c. collateral heir
d. non-lineal descendant

7. Distributees are
a. persons named in an individual's will.
b. all descendants of a decedent.
c. all living descendants and ancestors of a decedent.
d. those persons entitled to inherit from a decedent pursuant to the laws of intestacy.

8. Which of the following would be property of a decedent's estate?
a. a totten trust account.
b. the family Bible.
c. his home, owned by him and his surviving spouse as tenants by the entireties.
d. 100 shares of stock in his name only.

9. Dick died intestate. Who has the primary right to be appointed administrator of his estate?
a. his mother.
b. his surviving spouse.
c. his adult son.
d. his brother.

10. Who is eligible to serve as an administrator of an estate?
a. a convicted felon.
b. the decedent's 17 year old daughter.
c. the decedent's mother, who has been declared incompetent.
d. none of the above.

True or False:

1.___T__If a will omits some item of the decedent's property, and the will does not contain a residuary clause, then that item will pass by the laws of intestacy.

2.___F__The laws of intestate distribution are basically the same in all 50 states.

3.___F__Paul's grandmother is his lineal descendant.

4.___T__Amy's grandmother is in the 3rd degree of consanguinity to her.

5.___F__The distributees of a decedent are those persons named to inherit in his or her will.

6.___T__The laws of intestacy in New York no longer use the per stirpes method of distribution.

7.___T__A distribution by representation creates equality among those distributees who are in the same degree of consanguinity from the decedent.

8.___F___Property payable to a third party on the death of the decedent is considered part of the decedent's estate.

9.___T___The family Bible, domestic animals and housekeeping items are all examples of exempt property.

10.___F___New York does not have a statutory scheme establishing an order of priority as to who may serve as administrator of a decedent's estate.

Essay/Short Answers
Grandma Jean died last month without a will. Her husband, Grandpa Al, predeceased her. Jean and Al had 5 children, Anna, Bill, Cheryl, Denise and Evan. Bill and Cheryl predeceased Jean, so at Jean's death, Anna, Denise and Evan survived. At the time of Jean's death, Bill had three living children, Larry, Lynn and Lauren, and Cheryl had one living child, Randy. Jean has no other descendants.

a. Who will inherit Jean's assets in a "by representation" jurisdiction, and what will each share be? Explain.

- **Step 1: Go to the nearest generation with living descendants and divide by the number of persons (Jean and Al had 5 children), so each of their living children, Anna, Denise and Evan will receive 1/5th of the estate.**
- **Step 2: Combine the shares of the deceased children (Bill and Cheryl = 2/5ths).**
- **Step 3: Divide 2/5ths by the number of persons in the next generation (4).**
- **Each of Larry, Lynn, Lauren and Randy will receive 2/5ths x 1/4th of the estate = 2/20ths or 1/10th.**

b. Who will inherit Jean's assets in a "per stirpes" jurisdiction, and what will each share be? Explain.

- **Step 1: Go to the nearest generation with living descendants and divide by the number of persons (5), so that each of their living children, Anna, Denise and Evan will receive 1/5th of the estate.**
- **Step 2: Cheryl and Bill are each allocated 1/5th to pass to their descendants**
- **Bill has three children so each of them will receive 1/5th x 1/3rd of the estate = 1/15th.**
- **Cheryl has one child so he will receive her 1/5th share.**

c. Who will inherit Jean's assets in a "per capita" jurisdiction, and what will each share be? Explain.

- **Step 1: Go to the nearest generation with living descendants and divide by the number of living descendants.**
- **Step 2: each of Anna, Denise and Evan will receive 1/3rd of the estate.**
- **The children of Bill and Cheryl will receive nothing.**

Chapter 3
Status

Multiple Choice

1.Bill died and Mary claims to be his wife, although his children state that she was never married to him. What forms of proof are acceptable for Mary to prove her status as a surviving spouse?
a. proof that she and Bill entered into a common law marriage in Georgia.
b. a marriage license from New York.
c. a marriage license from Nevada.
d. all of the above.

2. Which of the following will **NOT** disqualify a spouse from inheriting through intestacy laws?
a. if the spouse abandoned the decedent.
b. if the spouse waived all rights in the decedent's estate in a prenuptial agreement.
c. if the spouse failed to support the decedent when able to do so.
d. if the decedent and his spouse were legally separated at the time of his death.

3. In general, an adopted child
a. will inherit from his biological parents.
b. will inherit from his adoptive parents only if his biological parents are deceased.
c. will inherit in a class gift ("to all my children") in his adoptive parents' wills as if he were their biological child.
d. will only inherit in his adoptive parents' wills if he is named specifically.

4. A child born after the date of his parent's will but before the death of the parent is a(n)
a. pretermitted child.
b. posthumous child.
c. omitted child.
d. unfortunate child

5. The decedent had two living daughters at the time of his death, and a son born six months after his death. His will leaves a class gift "to my children". Who will receive this gift?
a. All three children, equally.
b. His daughters only.
c. His son only.
d. the gift will be void.

6. Bill's will left most of his estate to his wife. Four years later Bill and his wife divorced, although Bill never changed his will. When he dies, what will happen?
a. his ex-wife inherits under the will.
b. the will is considered void.
c. the provisions in the will are given effect as if Bill's ex-wife had predeceased him.
d. his ex-wife only inherits under the will if she has not remarried.

7. A posthumous child is
a. a child omitted from a will.
b. a child born alive after her father's death.
c. a child born outside of wedlock.
d. a child who dies at birth.

8. Linda had a baby, Michael, when she was a teenager and ran away, leaving Michael with her mother, Lois, who adopted him. Many years later, Lois died.
a. Michael cannot inherit from Lois.
b. Michael will inherit from Lois as her grandson.
c. Michael will inherit from Lois as both her son and grandson.
d. Michael will inherit from Lois as her son.

9. Donna and Frank had a baby, Emma, when they were 16. Donna raised Emma as a single mother, although Frank and Donna did execute an acknowledgement of paternity according to the Public Health Law, and Frank openly acknowledged Emma as his daughter. Unfortunately, Frank's parents never accepted Emma, and only considered the two children of Frank's married sister as their grandchildren. When Frank's father died, he left a class gift of $100,000 "to my grandchildren". What does Emma receive?
a. nothing.
b. $100,000.
c. $50,000.
d. $33,333.33.

10. Vince is 34, and is the son of 84 year old Ruth, a rich socialite. He sneaks arsenic into her yogurt every morning and eventually she becomes sick and dies. Vince is convicted of murder. Who can inherit Ruth's estate?
a. Vince and his 10 year old son, Ethan.
b. Ethan, but not Vince.
c. Vince but not Ethan.
d. neither Vince nor Ethan.

True or False

1.__F__Because common law marriages are not valid in New York, New York will not recognize a common law marriage that is valid in another state for purposes of determining a person's status as a surviving spouse.

2.___T___Common forms of voluntary waiver of rights as a surviving spouse include a prenuptial agreement, postnuptial agreement and separation agreement.

3.___F___A person will lose his status as a surviving spouse if he abandoned his wife for 20 years, even if he returns home for the final 6 months of his wife's life.

4.___T___Disqualification of a spouse for failure to support requires a showing that the decedent looked to the spouse for support, the spouse had the means to support, and the spouse failed to support.

5.___F___If John fails to revise his will after his divorce, his ex-wife will be appointed executor of his estate if she was named executor in his will.

6.___F___Adopted children generally inherit from both their biological and adoptive families.

7.___T___A posthumous child generally will inherit from her decedent father as if she had been born in his lifetime.

8.___T___A testator may, in his will, specifically disinherit any child born after the date of the will.

9.___F___A child born outside of wedlock cannot inherit from her father unless specifically named in his will.

10.___F___The Surrogate's Court will routinely order posthumous DNA testing of a decedent any time paternity is at issue.

Essay/Short Answers

Mike and Paula have a son, Myles. Mike and Paula decide that parenting is "not their thing", so they leave baby Myles with Mike's sister, Jan, and take off for a commune. Jan and her husband adopt Myles, and Myles has no contact with his biological parents. Mike dies at the commune. The applicable intestacy statute reads as follows: "An adopted child may inherit from his or her biological parents if: (1) the person who adopted the child is either (a) married to the child's biological parent or (b) is the child's biological grandparent, or (c) is a descendant of the child's biological grandparent, and (2) the decedent is either (a) the child's biological grandparent, or (b) is a descendant of the child's biological grandparent."

a. Will Myles inherit from Mike? Explain your answer.

> **Myles will inherit from Mike because (1) the person who adopted Myles is a descendant of his biological grandparent, and (2) the decedent, Mike, was a descendant of Myles biological grandparent.**

84

b. If Myles will inherit from Mike, will he be considered his son (the biological relationship) or his nephew (his adoptive mother is Mike's sister)?   Explain.

Myles will be considered his son. If the adopted child is related to the decedent both biologically and by adoption, he can only inherit by way of the biological relationship unless the decedent is his adoptive parent. Since Mike was not his adoptive parent, he will inherit from him through their biological relationship.

c. If Myles had died instead of Mike, would Mike and Paula inherit from Myles? Explain.

Mike would not inherit from Myles. The rules permitting adopted children to inherit from their biological parents do not work both ways, so that the biological parents cannot inherit from the child.

Chapter 4
The New York Elective Share Statute

Multiple Choice

1. The purpose of the elective share statute is
a. to allow a large recovery by a spouse.
b. to limit inheritance by a testator's children.
c. to prevent a testator from disinheriting a spouse.
d. to provide more work for estate lawyers.

2. Paul died on November 12, 2005, and Letters Testamentary were issued by the Monroe County Surrogate's Court to his executor on March 6, 2006. If his wife chooses her elective share, she must file a Notice of Election by:
a. November 12, 2007.
b. March 6, 2007.
c. May 12, 2006.
d. September 6, 2006.

3. Designated lifetime transfers which are subject to a surviving spouse's elective share are called
a. lifetime substitutes.
b. inter vivos transfers.
c. elective share additions.
d. testamentary substitutes.

4. A surviving spouse must file a Notice of Election for an elective share with:
a. the decedent's executor and the appropriate Surrogate's Court.
b. the appropriate Surrogate's Court only.
c. the decedent's executor only.
d. the Recorder of Deeds.

5. John died with an estate valued at $5,000,000, although he left only $10,000 to his wife, Carol. Carol is only 25 years old, and her mother is outraged, so she plans to file a Notice of Election to claim Carol's elective share, because Carol refuses to do this.
a. this is proper as Carol's parents or siblings may claim the elective share for her.
b. this is improper as only Carol can claim the elective share.
c. this is proper if Carol's mother can show that John hid assets from Carol.
d. this is improper if Carol has sufficient funds to support herself.

6. What are the requirements for a voluntary waiver of the elective share?
a. only that it be in writing.
b. that it be in writing, signed by the maker, and acknowledged in the manner required for recording deeds.
c. the waiver may be oral, so long as there are witnesses.
d. the elective share may not be waived voluntarily.

7. What is a gift causa mortis?
a. a gift that so overwhelms the recipient that he or she dies.
b. a gift in anticipation of the death of the giver.
c. a belated birthday gift.
d. a gift that has no real value.

8. Money on deposit in a banking organization in the depositor's name in trust for another person is known as a(n)
a. joint savings account.
b. trust deposit.
c. totten trust account.
d. irrevocable gift.

9. Authority given by a donor to a donee to direct the disposition of certain property is known as a
a. power to direct.
b. power of appointment.
c. donative power.
d. power of disposition.

10. In addition to the surviving spouse, which of the following may exercise the right of election when authorized by the court?
a. the guardian of the property of an infant.
b. the committee of an incompetent spouse.
c. the guardian ad litem for the surviving spouse.
d. all of the above.

True or False.

1.__F__Under the current law, only property of the decedent located in New York is subject to the elective share.

2.__F__The elective share is only available to surviving wives, not husbands.

3.__T__ The right to elect the elective share may only be exercised during the lifetime of the surviving spouse.

4.__F__The surviving spouse may exercise the elective share by oral notice to the executor.

5.__T__The Surrogate's Court has the power to extend the time for a surviving spouse to exercise the elective share.

6.__T__A spouse may voluntarily waive the right to the elective share during his or her lifetime.

7.__F__The fiduciary of a surviving spouse may exercise the elective share on his or her behalf.

8.__F__The Surrogate's Court may not relieve a surviving spouse of a default in exercising the elective share.

9.__T__The original notice of election must be filed with the Surrogate's Court that issued letters to the decedent's fiduciary.

10.__F__Testamentary substitutes are transfers made by the decedent to his spouse only.

Essay/Short Answers

The decedent's will left $1,100,000 to his friend and $100,000 to his wife. Funeral, estate administration expenses and debts were $50,000. The decedent also left a totten trust for his daughter in the amount of $50,000. The decedent's spouse decides to claim her elective share. How much will she receive? Show your work in detail.

Step 1: calculate the value of the net estate subject to the elective share:

$1,200,000 = assets disposed of by will
+   0 = intestate property
+   50,000 = testamentary substitutes (totten trust)
$1,250,000 = gross estate subject to elective share
-    50,000 = debts
$1,200,000 = net estate subject to elective share

Step 2: calculate the greater of $50,000 or 1/3rd of the net estate.
1/3rd of $1,200,000 = $400,000 which is greater than $50,000

Step 3: Subtract disposition by will
$400,000
-100,000
$300,000 = net elective share amount

Chapter 5
Probate of Wills

Multiple Choice

1. The clause appearing at the end of the will where the witnesses certify that the will was executed in accordance with the statutory requirements is the
a. self-proving affidavit.
b. attestation clause
c. nuncupative clause.
d. codicil

2. In order for a will to be validly executed, the testator's signature must appear
a. at the beginning of the will.
b. on each page of the will.
c. at the end of the will.
d. in the margin of the will.

3. In New York, an attesting witness
a. must be at least 18 years of age.
b. must be at least 21 years of age.
c. must only be of an age to sufficiently understand his or her actions and the formality of the will execution.
d. must be at least 25 years of age.

4. The testator's act of declaring an instrument to be his or her will is called
a. validation.
b. execution.
c. self-proving.
d. publication

5. Which of the following persons could make a valid nuncupative will?
a. an army chaplain accompanying army troops on night patrol in Iraq.
b. a marine on home leave in Cleveland.
c. an army recruit in training at a time when the United States in not engaged in any war or armed conflict.
d. a navy captain on shore leave in Hawaii.

6. If a will does not have a 1406 self-proving affidavit, and the witnesses are alive and available,
a. it will be admitted to probate so long as no one objects.
b. the testimony of the attesting witnesses will be taken before the court.
c. it may not be admitted to probate under any circumstances and the decedent's property will pass by intestacy.
d. it will be admitted to probate so long as it was validly executed.

7. A will that is more than thirty years old is known as
a. an ancient will.
b. a holographic will.
c. a nuncupative will.
d. a self-proving will.

8. Necessary parties to a probate proceeding include all BUT
a. the distributees of the decedent.
b. the person designated by the will as executor..
c. the person designated by the will as guardian of the decedent's minor children.
d. a friend who is to receive a bequest under the will.

9. Each necessary party to a probate proceeding must be served with process, known as a
a. probate notice.
b. citation.
c. surrogate service.
d. will notice.

10. When the probate of a will is delayed, the court will may appoint _____ to protect the estate.
a. an administrator.
b. a surrogate referee.
c. an estate protector.
d. a temporary executor.

True or False

1. __F__ In order to be valid, the testator must sign the will with his or her full name.

2. __T__ A person other than the testator may sign a will in the name of the testator provided that it is done in the presence of the testator and at his or her direction.

3. __F__ The testator must sign the will in the presence of the attesting witnesses.

4. __T__ A handwritten will is admissible to probate as a duly executed instrument provided that it satisfies the requirements of the EPTL.

5. __F__ Admiral Marks made a valid holographic will while onboard a United States battleship cruising the South Pacific Ocean in June, 2001. When he died six months later in a surfing accident while on shore leave in Maui, his will was no longer valid.

6. __F__ Even though a will has a1406 self-proving affidavit, testimony of the attesting witnesses is still required.

7. __F__ Any small mistake by the scrivener of a will results in denial of probate.

8.___T___It is a Class E felony for a person to destroy a will with the intent to defraud.

9.___F___Failure to provide notice of probate to all persons named in a propounded will, even if they are not distributees of the testator, is jurisdictional and will void the probate proceedings.

10.___F___An executor named in a will is always required to file a bond as a prerequisite to the issuance of letters testamentary.

Short Answers

1. One of the firm's clients is in a nursing home and is too weak to sign her will. She wants her daughter to guide her hand as she signs the will. Can she still have a duly executed will? What advice should we give her?

> **Yes, she can still have a validly executed will, and her daughter may assist her in signing it. The attestation clause should state that her signature was made with her daughter's assistance, at her request.**

2. The testator writes a will and signs it in the privacy of his home, and two days later brings it to his attorney. What steps can be taken to make this will duly executed?

> **This will can still be valid and duly executed if two attesting witnesses attest to the testator's signature at his request and each witness signs his or her name and residence address to an attestation clause within 30 days of each other.**

3. The testator's will leaves half of his entire estate to his daughter. The attesting witnesses are his daughter, his attorney and her secretary. There is no 1406 affidavit. At the time of the testator's death, his attorney is also deceased. Is the bequest to his daughter valid?

> **No, the bequest is not valid as the testimony of the daughter is necessary to prove the will. However, as she is a distributee, she will receive the lesser of the bequest or her intestate share of her father's estate.**

Chapter 6
Contested Probate Proceedings

Multiple Choice

1. What is the purpose of a no contest or in terrorem clause in a will?
a. it is a provision that says that no one can contest the will.
b. it is a provision in a will that provides that if a beneficiary contests the will, any testamentary disposition to that beneficiary will be void.
c. it is a provision stating that the executor may not contest the will.
d. it is a provision against terrorism.

2. Courts will presume that a will was duly executed when
a. it is handwritten.
b. no one objects to the will.
c. the execution of the will was supervised by a lawyer or the will contains an attestation clause.
d. the testator is fluent in English.

3. If a testator is not fluent in English
a. it is necessary that the will be read to the testator verbatim in his or her native language.
b. the will can never be valid.
c. this has no effect on the validity of the will.
d. the will is valid if it is clear that the testator knew and understood the will's contents.

4. Evidence showed that the testator firmly believed that the moon was inhabited by green space creatures who made frequent visits to the earth. This is an example of
a. a delusion.
b. a lucid interval.
c. a religious belief
d. an eccentricity

5. Even if a testator is suffering from a mental disability, his will may still be valid if evidence shows that he executed the will during
a. an insane delusion.
b. a time when he was medicated.
c. a lucid interval.
d. dinner.

6. In matters concerning testamentary capacity, non-attesting lay witnesses
a. cannot testify about anything relating to the testator's mental capacity.
b. may testify as to acts and declarations of the testator and state the impression that these acts and declarations produced upon their minds.
c. may express an opinion as to the mental capacity of the testator.
d. may not testify at all.

7. Which of the following is NOT required to prove undue influence?
a. motive
b. opportunity
c. the actual exercise of undue influence.
d. old age or infirmity of the testator.

8. An individual authorized by another to act in his place and stead, either for some particular purpose, of for the transaction of business in general, not of a legal character, is known as
a. a guardian.
b. a trustee.
c. an attorney in fact.
d. a beneficiary.

9. If the testator's sister told her that the testator's son had cheated her in the family business for the purpose of making the testator change her will, and this was not true, this would be an example of
a. undue influence.
b. lack of testamentary capacity.
c. mistake.
d. fraud.

10. When a citation is issued in respect of a petition for probate of a will, an interested party may object
a. on or before the return date stated in the citation.
b. within 30 days of the citation.
b. within 60 days of the citation.
d. within 90 days of the citation.

True or False.

1.__T__The proponent of a will has the burden of proving that the will was duly executed and that the testator had testamentary capacity on the date of execution.

2.__T__Executing a will requires less mental capacity than any other legal instrument.

3.__F__If a testator is old and infirm, he or she always lacks testamentary capacity.

4.___F___Attesting witnesses to a will may not render an opinion in court as to the mental capacity of a decedent to execute a will.

5.___T___It is not undue influence if a will is the result of affection or gratitude.

6.___F___Undue influence may never be proved by circumstantial evidence.

7.___T___The fact that a beneficiary under the will occupied a confidential relationship with the testator does not, in and of itself, create a presumption of undue influence.

8.___F___Fraud in the execution of a will is generally easy to prove.

9.___T___Any person whose interest in property or in the estate of a testator would be adversely affected by the admission of the will to probate may file objections to the probate of the will.

10.___T___Once objections to probate have been properly filed, the parties may proceed with discovery in accordance with the NY Civil Practice Law and Rules.

Short Answers

1. A will dated 2004 is offered for probate, leaving the testator's entire estate to his son and his daughter. A prior will of the testator left most of his estate to his son and daughter, but also included bequests to his grandson and a local charity. Who of the following has standing to object to the 2004 will? Explain.

> **a. The testator's grandson? The grandson has standing because his interest under the prior will is adversely affected by the 2004 will.**
> **b. The testator's sister? The sister does not have standing because she has no interest that is adversely affected by the 2004 will.**
> **c. The local charity? The local charity has standing because its interest under the prior will is adversely affected by the 2004 will.**

2. The testator's will contained a bequest of $20,000 to his brother, and an in terrorem clause relating to that bequest. The brother filed objections, but one month later withdrew his objections. Is his bequest void due to the in terrorem clause?

> **The bequest is probably still valid. Courts have held that merely filing objections and then withdrawing them does not constitute a sufficient contest to void a bequest pursuant to an in terrorem clause.**

3. The testator comes to your office to execute his will, accompanied by his daughter, who explains that her father is becoming forgetful and has periods of disorientation. Can he still validly execute a will?

Probably yes. The execution of a will requires less mental capacity than any other legal action. So long as he executes the will during a lucid interval, it should be valid.

Chapter 7
Revocation of Wills

Multiple Choice

1. When a testator obliterates her 1997 will with the words, "see will dated January 14, 2002", and at her death it is determined that the January 14, 2000 will was not duly executed,
a. the January 14th will may be deemed duly executed.
b. testamentary effect may be given to the earlier will, despite the testator's supposed revocation.
c. the testator's estate will pass by intestacy.
d. the testator's heirs may choose which will to be probated.

2. If the testator's will contained the words "revoked" in the margin, followed by his initials,
a. the revocation is effective as it is in the testator's handwriting.
b. the revocation is not effective as it is not witnessed or attested.
c. the revocation is effective if it can be proved that the testator was competent at the time he wrote the words on his will.
d. the revocation is not effective because wills cannot be revoked unless replaced with another will.

3. If the testator writes a will in 2000 and writes a later will in 2003, but the 2003 will says nothing about revoking the prior will,
a. the prior will is be revoked by implication if the terms of the two wills are inconsistent.
b. the earlier will remains valid.
c. the wills are construed together.
d. neither will is valid.

4. Which of the following facts would support a revocation by obliteration?
a. the testator writes the words "revoked" next to his signature.
b. the testator writes the words "null and void" across two of six general bequests.
c. the testator marks an "X" over each page of the will, affecting the entire instrument.
d. the testator crosses out a specific bequest.

5. Shortly before her death, the testator asked her son to burn her will.
a. This is not an effective revocation as it was not done by the testator.
b. This is an effective revocation so long as the testator requested that it be done.
c. This is an effective revocation only if the testator requested that it be done and it was done in her presence.
d. This is an effective revocation only if the testator requested that it be done, it was done in her presence, and was witnessed by two additional persons.

6. Re-execution and re-attestation of a prior will is known as
a. republication.
b. dependent relative revocation.
c. revocation by implication.
d. will revival.

7. The theory that comes from the presumption that the testator would prefer that his or her property to pass by the terms of a will rather than by intestacy, and so revives a prior will when a later will turns out to be invalid, even though the later will purports to revoke the prior will, is called
a. revival.
b. alteration.
c. dependent relative revocation.
d. revocation by implication.

8. The best and most common way for a testator to revoke his will is
a. by a handwritten note of the testator.
b. by express language in a subsequent will.
c. by noting in the margin that it has been revoked.
d. by telling his family that the will is revoked.

9. If the testator wishes to revoke his will by a subsequent writing
a. the writing should be executed with the formalities for executing and attesting a valid will.
b. the writing need not be witnessed if it is signed.
c. the testator cannot revoke a will by a subsequent writing.
d. the writing must be completely in the testator's handwriting.

10. During the lifetime of the testator
a. her will cannot be revoked.
b. her will can be revoked only if there is a change in her life circumstances (death of spouse, birth of child, etc.).
c. her will can be revoked only if the beneficiaries under the will consent.
d. her will can be revoked at will.

True or False

1.__F__In order to revoke a will a testator can have less mental capacity than is needed to make a will.

2.__T__If the testator's last will was known to be in his possession and it cannot be found in his personal effects after his death, it is presumed that he revoked the will.

3.__F__A will may be partially revoked by a physical act.

4.__F__The revocation of a codicil revives the provisions of a will that were revoked by the codicil.

5.__T__The revocation of a will revokes all codicils to that will.

6.__T__A person who is authorized to make a holographic will may also revise a prior will by holographic declaration.

7.__T__If a will is last known to be in the possession of the testator and at his death is found in his personal effects cut or otherwise mutilated, there is a presumption that the testator intended to revoke the will.

8.__F__A will can be revoked by an oral statement of the testator.

9.__F__If the testator has periods of confusion and disorientation, he does not under any circumstances have mental capacity to revoke his will.

10.__T__If the testator destroys his will on the basis of a fraud, the will may still be admitted to probate if the will was properly executed and the fraud can be proved.

Short Answers.

1. The testator became angry at his brother and crossed off his bequest to his brother in his will. Is this valid to revoke only this bequest?

> **No, revocation by physical act is only valid to revoke the entire will, not a part of it.**

2. What evidence can be introduced to show that an elderly and disoriented testator had the capacity to revoke his will?

> **Evidence that at the time of the revocation, the testator appeared lucid and understood that the instrument he was revoking was his will, that he understood its provisions, and that he desired to revoke it.**

3. If the testator is physically disabled, and he instructs his son to burn his will, is this a valid revocation?

> **Yes, if the son burns the will at his father's request, in his presence, and in the presence of at least two other persons.**

Chapter 8
Joint and Mutual Wills

Multiple Choice

1. Barb and Bert execute mutual wills, leaving all of their property to each other, and if one or the other does not survive, to their son and daughter in equal shares. Barb dies first and Bert changes his will to leave more to his son. When Bert dies, will their daughter succeed in having her father's will changed so that she and her brother receive equal shares?
a. yes, because it was clearly their parents' intent that they receive equal shares.
b. no, because mutual wills are not generally contracts that the survivor will not change the will.
c. yes, because mutual wills can never be changed.
d. no, because contracts to make a will are void as against public policy.

2. A single testamentary document that represents the wills of two persons is a
a. mutual will.
b. two party will.
c. holographic will.
d. joint will.

3. A contract to make a will must be proved
a. beyond a reasonable doubt.
b. by clear and convincing evidence.
c. by a slight preponderance of evidence.
d. contracts to make a will are void in New York.

4. A contract to make a joint will and not to revoke that will
a. can only be established by an express statement in the will itself.
b. may be established by any writing, signed by the testator.
c. may be proved without a writing if there is sufficient evidence of the contract.
d. may be implied from the terms of the will.

5. If Mr. and Mrs. Jones have a contract to make a will, and after the death of Mrs. Jones, Mr. Jones revises his will, when Mr. Jones dies
a. his new will can be admitted to probate and the intended beneficiaries of the will contract have no redress.
b. his new will can be admitted to probate but the intended beneficiaries of the will contract have a claim against his estate.
c. his new will cannot be admitted to probate.
d. his new will is automatically void.

6. Mr. and Mrs. Smith have a contract to make a will, leaving their property in equal amounts to their three children. After Mr. Smith's death, Mrs. Smith transfers substantial assets to their youngest child.

a. this transfer is permissible as it is not a transfer by will.

b. when Mrs. Smith dies, the other two Smith children will have a claim against Mrs. Smith's estate for a proportional amount of the inter vivos transfers by Mrs. Smith.

c. Mrs. Smith's will may not be admissible to probate.

d. when Mrs. Smith dies the two older children have a claim against the youngest child directly, but not against Mrs. Smith's estate.

True or False.

1.___T___Contracts that limit the ability of a person to freely dispose of his or her property, including dispositions by will, are generally disfavored by the courts.

2.___F___In New York, a contract to make a testamentary provision may be oral if proved by sufficient evidence.

3.___T___The person who claims the existence of a contract to make a will has the burden of proving such a contract.

4.___T___A party to a will contract may still use his property for his own benefit during his lifetime.

5.___F___The only remedy for the breach of a will contract is damages.

6.___T___The existence of mutual wills with reciprocal provisions does not, in and of itself, prove a contract to make a will.

7.___T___Mutual wills between a husband and wife are very common.

8.___F___Even if a contract to make a will exists, after the death of one party the other party may revise his or her will for good cause.

9.___F___If a husband and wife are parties to a contract to make a will, after the death of one spouse the other spouse is prohibited from giving any inter vivos gifts whatsoever to one of the will beneficiaries.

10.___T___If assets are transferred inter vivos in violation of a will contract, the court may direct that the assets be restored to the estate.

Short Answers

1.Mr. and Mrs. Willard make mutual wills with valid contractual provisions. The following year Mrs. Willard amends her will. What should she do to make certain that the amendment is valid?

> **She should provide notice of the amendment to Mr. Willard. If he fails to object, the amendment will be valid.**

2. Mr. and Mrs. Johnson are parties to a will contract in which they agree to leave their assets in equal shares to their two daughters and to Mrs. Johnson's son from an earlier marriage. Following Mr. Johnson's death Mrs. Johnson transfers her residence to her son. Has she done anything wrong? Explain. After her death, discuss any possible remedies her daughters will have.

> **Mrs. Johnson has made an inter vivos gift in violation of the will contract. Following her death, the daughters may sue her estate for breach of contract. They may seek damages, restoration of property to her estate, or a constructive trust on estate assets.**

3. Mr. and Mrs. Lee have mutual wills with reciprocal provisions. The wills themselves say nothing about being irrevocable, but the Lees have told their four children on numerous occasions, with witnesses, that they intend to leave their assets to the children in substantially equal shares. When they die, the oldest daughter's bequest is substantially more valuable than those to her siblings because shares of stock she is to inherit have tripled in value. Do her siblings have any recourse?

> **No, because the mere existence of mutual wills with reciprocal provisions does not create a contract to make a will. This can only be done in a clear and convincing writing, supported by consideration.**

Chapter 9
Trusts

Multiple Choice

1. A trust imposed by the court to prevent a party from being unjustly enriched is
a. an enrichment trust.
b. a testamentary trust.
c. an inter vivos trust.
d. a constructive trust.

2. In a trust, the same person CANNOT be both
a. sole settlor and sole trustee.
b. sole settlor and sole beneficiary.
c. sole trustee and sole beneficiary.
d. all of the above are prohibited.

3. The settlor of an inter vivos trust must have
a. only the same capacity necessary to make a will.
b. the same capacity necessary to make a contract, which is more than is required to make a will.
c. less capacity than is necessary to make a will.
d. no capacity – anyone, no matter how incompetent, may set up an inter vivos trust.

4. Which person is eligible to serve as a trustee in New York?
a. a convicted felon
b. a sixteen year old.
c. a person who has been declared mentally incompetent.
d. none of the above.

5. If Marge is both the sole trustee and sole beneficiary of a trust, this results in
a. a legal and enforceable trust.
b. merger of the legal and equitable interests and an end of the trust.
c. a court request for a new trustee.
d. an explosion of the trust.

6. Ken has no children. He establishes a trust for the benefit of his children, then grandchildren, then great grandchildren. This trust
a. is legal and enforceable.
b. is legal and enforceable only if it is set up as a testamentary trust.
c. violates the rule against perpetuities and is not legal or enforceable.
d. is legal and enforceable only if it is irrevocable.

7. A bank account titled "Audrey, in trust for Clara" is an example of
a. a constructive trust.
b. a resulting trust.
c. a spendthrift trust.
d. a totten trust.

8. A trust which gives the trustee authority to accumulate or distribute income, principal or both among the beneficiaries in varying amounts as needed is called a
a. sprinkling trust.
b. resulting trust.
c. totten trust.
d. spendthrift trust.

9. A spendthrift trust is useful when the beneficiary
a. is wealthy.
b. is unable to control his or her spending.
c. is disabled.
d. is elderly.

10. The Cy Pres Doctrine
a. makes charitable trusts illegal.
b. tries to give effect to charitable trusts whenever possible.
c. causes a trust to arise by operation of law when the trust ends without a remainderman.
d. provides that a trust cannot last forever.

True or False

1.__T__Although a trustee is essential to the administration of a trust, failure to name a trustee will not cause the trust to fail.

2.__F__If the language creating a trust is ambiguous, the court will infer that a trust has been created.

3.__F__A statement by the grantor that she is going to create a trust is sufficient to create the trust.

4.__T__A holder of an estate for years in real property may transfer that property in trust.

5.__F__Any professional corporation is eligible to serve as a trustee.

6.__F__A trust is merged and therefore invalid if the same person is the trustee and one of the three beneficiaries.

7.__T__A person appointed in a will as trustee of a testamentary trust may renounce his or her appointment.

8.___T___A trustee can only resign from office if permitted by the court to do so or by following the resignation procedures set forth in the trust instrument.

9.___F___If the grantor transfers $500,000 in trust and directs the trustee to pay the income to A for life and the remainder to B, B has a contingent future interest.

10.___T___To create a life insurance trust, the grantor either assigns the policy on his life to the trustee, or designates the trustee as beneficiary of the proceeds of the life insurance policy.

Short Answers/Terminology.

1. The person who places property in the trust and creates the trust is the **grantor or settlor.**

2. The recipient of income produced from trust property is the **trust beneficiary.**

3. The capital or assets placed in the trust is the **trust principal**.

4. A trust created under the will of a decedent is a **testamentary trust.**

5. The property placed into a trust is the **trust res or corpus.**

6. The recipient of the trust property is the **trust beneficiary.**

7. The recipient of the balance of the trust at the conclusion of the trust term is the **trust remainderman.**

8. A trust created during the lifetime of the grantor is **an inter vivos trust.**

9. A trust created in express terms, either oral or written, is **an express trust**.

10. The balance of the trust on hand at the end of the trust term is the **remainder.**

Chapter 10
Gift Transactions

Multiple Choice

1. Kim opened a joint bank account with survivorship rights with her sister Jill and deposited $1000.00 into the account.
a. Kim is presumed to have made a gift to Jill of $1000.
b. The entire $1000 is presumed to be Kim's.
c. Kim is presumed to have made a gift to Jill of $500.
d. It is not possible for sisters to have joint bank accounts with a right of survivorship.

2. Leigh wore her mother's pearls to a wedding in 1995, and still had the pearls in her jewelry box in 2005 when her mother died. Leigh's sister Martha claims that the pearls should be included in her mother's estate, but Leigh says they were a gift.
a. since Leigh has had possession of the pearls for 10 years, it is clear that they were a gift.
b. Leigh will have to prove that her mother intended to give her the pearls.
c. Leigh can prove that the pearls were a gift because she has a note from her mother saying that "I want you to have these pearls when I die".
d. Transfers between family members are never gifts.

3. Mike is the guardian for his father, who is incompetent. Mike claims that his father gave him his clock collection. Mike's sister Lou says that Mike exercised undue influence over their father to get the collection.
a. Lou has the burden of proving undue influence.
b. Since Mike is his father's guardian, there is a presumption that all of his actions are in his father's best interest.
c. Since Mike is his father's guardian, Mike has the burden of proving that there was no undue influence on his part.
d. Guardians are free to take any property belonging to their wards.

4. Ralph gave his grandson shares of stock, and had the stock reregistered in his grandson's name. This is an example of
a. constructive delivery.
b. physical delivery.
c. alternative delivery.
d. fraudulent delivery.

5. Sally gave Nick the keys to a storage locker containing her bicycle.
a. This proves that Sally intended to give Nick her bike.
b. This is not sufficient to show that Sally intended to give Nick the bike.
c. This will only prove intent to make a gift if Sally and Nick are related.
d. This will prove intent to make a gift unless the bike is obviously a woman's bike.

6. A gift made in contemplation of death is a
a. deathbed gift
b. dying gift.
c. gift causa mortis
d. gift rigor mortis.

7. A person appointed by the court to oversee the property or financial interests of another, who is in need of protection, is a
a. conservator.
b. trustee.
c. protector.
d. administrator.

8. If a gift is not delivered to the donee until after the death of the donor
a. the transfer will be considered testamentary.
b. the transfer will still be an effective inter vivos gift.
c. the transfer will fail as an inter vivos gift.
d. the transfer will be considered an effective inter vivos gift only if there is written proof of the donor's intent to make a gift.

9. The donor's acceptance of an inter vivos gift
a. can only be express, not implied.
b. must be made immediately.
c. is never presumed.
d. is presumed when the gift is valuable to the donee.

10. A valid gift causa mortis
a. can be made even if the donor recovers, so long as he or she believed that death was imminent at the time of the gift.
b. is effective even if the gift is not delivered until after the donor's death.
c. requires all of the elements of a valid inter vivos gift.
d. can be made when the donor is well, if the donor dies within thirty days of the gift.

True or False.

1. ___F___. The burden of proving that a valid gift was made is on the donor.

2. ___T___. Registration of stock in joint names with right of survivorship is strong evidence of a decedent's donative intent with respect to the stock.

3. ___T___. In making a gift, it is not essential that the donor intend to transfer title and possession immediately, so long as it is established that the donee received title or the right of ownership immediately upon the making of a gift.

4. ___F___. Physical delivery is an essential element of a gift transfer.

5.___T__. Delivery of keys to a safe deposit box will be a sufficient delivery of the contents of the box where circumstances do not permit actual delivery of the box and the donor relinquishes dominion and control over the property in the box.

6.___F__. The deposit of items into a jointly leased safe deposit box always constitutes a gift of those items to the other owner of the box.

7.___F__. Acceptance by the donee is not necessary for a valid inter vivos gift.

8.___T__. Mere possession is not sufficient to establish proof of a gift.

9.___T__. There is a general presumption that every person is competent to make a gift, absent a showing to the contrary.

10.__F__. So long as physical possession of an item is in the possession of the alleged donee, a valid inter vivos gift will be presumed, even if there has not been a present transfer of ownership by the grantor.

Short Answers
Morris is 93 years old and has not been ruled incompetent, but is showing signs of dementia. He gave his model train collection to his grandson Bruce, but told Bruce that he would like to keep some of the trains at his house so that he can run them around the Christmas tree. He also told Bruce that if he does not take good care of the trains, he will take them back and give them to his granddaughter, Susan. Morris would have given them to Susan, but Bruce told him in no uncertain terms that he wants the trains, and that he would not continue to take Morris to his doctor's appointments and out to dinner if Morris does not give the trains to him.

1.. Does Morris's dementia mean than he cannot give a valid gift?
> **Although Morris's dementia is a concern, he has not been ruled incompetent, so it will be up to anyone objecting to prove incompetence. It is quite possible that he made the gift during a lucid interval.**

2. Can Morris give the trains to Bruce and keep them at his house?
> **One of the requirements of a valid gift is delivery, and Morris's refusal to deliver all of the trains to Bruce might affect the validity of the gift of those trains.**

3. Can Morris take the trains away from Bruce and give them to Susan?
> **No, for a valid gift the transfer must be irrevocable.**

4. What effect do Bruce's threats have on the validity of the gift?
> **Bruce has exercised undue influence over Morris and so the gift is not voluntary, rendering it void.**

Chapters 11 & 12
Jurisdiction and Power of the Surrogate's Court
Venue of Surrogate's Court Proceedings

Multiple Choice

1. Mrs. Ruiz lives in Buffalo but spends four months each winter at her beach condo in Texas. In January, she is domiciled in
a. New York.
b. Texas.
c. both New York and Texas.
d. She has no domicile.

2. Probate proceedings for Mr. Thompson's will are filed in both Ontario and Monroe Counties. Both counties have venue. Where will the case proceed?
a. the county where most of his heirs live.
b. the county where the proposed executor lives.
c. the county where the will was drafted.
d. the county where the proceedings were filed first.

3. Sally is the trustee of a lifetime trust created by Steve. Sally lives in Broome County, Steve lives in Erie County and the trust assets are in a bank in Westchester County. Which county has venue?
a. Broome County.
b. Erie County.
c. Westchester County.
d. all of the above.

4. Susan died domiciled in Albemarle County, North Carolina, but she had a lake home in Wayne County, New York and her parents live in Monroe County, New York. Which county has jurisdiction over her real property in Wayne County?
a. Albemarle County.
b. Wayne County
c. Monroe County
d. all of the above.

5. What New York Court has subject matter jurisdiction over all matters relating to a decedent's estate?
a. the Family Court.
b. the Supreme Court only.
c. the Surrogate's Court only.
d. both the Surrogate's Court and the Supreme Court.

6. Subject matter jurisdiction

a. can be waived if all parties consent.

b. is determined by each court at its own discretion.

c. is given to each court by the constitution or statute that creates the court.

d. can never be questioned.

7. Larry lives in Cook County, Illinois. While visiting his mother in Syracuse (Onondaga County) he was struck and killed by a bus. His estate wishes to pursue a wrongful death claim against the bus company. The wrongful death lawsuit should proceed in

a. Cook County, Illinois.

b. Onondaga County, New York.

c. either Cook County or Onondaga County.

d. any county in New York.

8. A second estate administration used to distribute real property of a nondomiciliary decedent who leaves real property in New York is called

a. a secondary administration.

b. an auxiliary administration

c. an ancillary administration.

d. a bonus administration.

9. Fred dies intestate domiciled in Texas but owns real property located in New York. What law will apply to determine which of his heirs will inherit the NY property?

a. Texas law.

b. New York law.

c. Either law that the court chooses to apply.

d. Whichever law will leave more to his surviving spouse.

10. Service of process in Surrogate's Court is usually by means of serving a

a. request for appearance.

b. court mandate.

c. citation.

d. surrogate's notice.

True or False

1.__F__If a court lacks subject matter jurisdiction over a proceeding, it can still hear and decide the issues in that proceeding if no party objects.

2.__F__The Surrogate's Court will have subject matter jurisdiction over a dispute between an estate beneficiary and his landlord, who attempted to attach a distribution to the beneficiary.

3.__T__The Surrogate's Court of any county in New York has subject matter jurisdiction over the estate of a decedent who was domiciled in New York at the time of her death.

4.__T__ The decision by the Surrogate's Court to exercise jurisdiction over the estate of a non-domiciliary is discretionary.

5.__F__ Only the Surrogate's Court in the county where trust assets are located has subject matter jurisdiction over a lifetime trust.

6.__T__ By receiving a legacy or property of an estate, a non-domiciliary legatee or distributee submits herself to the personal jurisdiction of the New York Surrogate's Court.

7.__T__ A competent adult may appear in a proceeding by his or her attorney.

8.__F__ A party can only make an appearance by actually appearing in a courtroom.

9.__F__ It is possible for an individual to be domiciled in two different states at the same time.

10.__T__ If the estate of a non-domiciliary decedent has a wrongful death cause of action against a New York domiciliary, the proper venue is the domicile of the New Yorker.

Terminology

1. The authority of a court to hear and determine issues is **subject matter jurisdiction.**

2. A person whose domicile is in the state of New York is a New York **domiciliary.**

3. If a person does not voluntarily appear in the Surrogate's Court, personal jurisdiction is generally obtained by serving **process.**

4. An infant may appear in a Surrogate Court proceeding by his or her **guardian** of property.

5. A corporation may appear in a Surrogate Court proceeding by its **attorney**.

6. An attorney appointed by the court to represent the interests of a person under disability is a **guardian ad litem.**

7. A person who is domiciled outside of the state of New York is a **non-domiciliary.**

8. The Surrogate's Court of any county has subject matter over the estate of a person domiciled outside of New York only if such person left a cause of action for wrongful death against someone domiciled in New York, or if such person left **property** in New York.

9. In order for a court order to be fully effective and binding, the court must obtain personal jurisdiction over all **necessary parties**.

10. The preferred method for service of process upon someone domiciled in New York is by **personal delivery**.

Short Answers

1. How can New York get personal jurisdiction over an out of state defendant?

New York can get personal jurisdiction over an out of state defendant if that defendant voluntarily comes to court in New York, or if that defendant has sufficient contacts with New York.

2. What is a Long Arm Statute?

A Long Arm Statute is a statute which allows a New York court to obtain personal jurisdiction over an out of state defendant on the basis of the defendant's conduct and actions in New York.

3. Jason is in the process of moving from New York to California. He has packed up all of his belongings in New York and is driving the truck to California. If he dies from an accident in Colorado, where is he domiciled at the time of his death? Explain.

At the time of his death, Jason's domicile will be either New York or California, depending on which state has more connections with him at the time of his death.

Chapter 13
Fiduciary Duties in Administering an Estate

Multiple Choice

1. Which of the following actions may a named executor take prior to the issuance of letters testamentary?
a. sell the decedent's residence.
b. distribute bequests to beneficiaries.
c. pay estate debts.
d. pay the decedent's reasonable funeral expenses.

2. Which of the following is considered an estate asset for collection purposes?
a. a totten trust account.
b. stock owned solely by the decedent.
c. life insurance proceeds from a policy on the life of the decedent, payable to a named beneficiary.
d. a joint bank account owned by the decedent and his surviving spouse.

3. Which of the following is NOT necessary to transfer registered securities into the name of the estate?
a. a letter of instruction with signature guaranteed.
b. a short form certificate of letters testamentary or letters of administration.
c. the stock certificates.
d. a letter from the issuer of the stock or security.

4. In valuing estate assets for the estate inventory, the fiduciary should use
a. the original purchase price.
b. the fair market value at the date of death.
c. the fair market value at the time of distribution.
d. whichever value the fiduciary chooses to use.

5. The first priority expense of an estate is
a. the decedent's funeral expenses.
b. the decedent's unpaid income taxes.
c. the decedent's secured creditors.
d. the administration expenses of the estate.

6. Which of the following non-testamentary property cannot be subject to the claims of estate creditors?
a. life insurance proceeds.
b. totten trust accounts.
c. joint bank accounts.
d. inter vivos trusts.

7. Income earned by the decedent prior to death but not yet reported for income tax purposes is known as
a. unreported income.
b. tentative income.
c. income in respect of a decedent.
d. capital gains.

8. If the decedent died on January 15, 2003, his federal estate tax return is due to be filed on
a. January 15, 2004.
b. April 15, 2004
c. October 15, 2003.
d. July 15, 2004.

9. Every fiduciary must file a list of estate assets called the
a. estate accounting.
b. estate inventory.
c. estate asset list.
d. estate advancement.

10. A proceeding to compel distribution may be commenced against an estate fiduciary
a. immediately upon the decedent's death.
b. 6 months following the decedent's death.
c. 7 months following the decedent's death.
d. one year following the decedent's death.

11. The amount of a fiduciary's commissions are based upon
a. the value of property received and paid during the fiduciary's administration.
b. the length of the estate administration.
c. the complexity of the estate administration.
d. the amount negotiated between the fiduciary and the estate beneficiaries.

12. The process whereby a fiduciary is found derelict in the performance of his duties and directed to make the estate whole for the resulting loss is called
a. restitution.
b. estate fines.
c. surcharging.
d. advancement.

True or False

1.___T__. A named executor has no authority to dispose of estate assets prior to being appointed by the court.

2.___T__. If the decedent's real property is specifically devised by her will, the executor's only duty is to confirm its existence and value it for estate tax purposes.

3.___F___. So long as there is no objection, the fiduciary may deposit estate assets into his or her personal bank account.

4.___T___. If the decedent's real property is sold soon after the decedent' death, the selling price may be the best indication of the property's fair market value.

5.___F___. The fiduciary never has a duty to invest estate assets.

6.___F___. A claim against an estate presented more than seven months after the decedent's death is invalid.

7.___T___. A fiduciary may not pay claims to himself or herself out of the decedent's estate until allowed by the court.

8.___T___. If a decedent was married at the time of her death, and would have been permitted to file a joint income tax return, then the executor may file a joint tax return with the surviving spouse so long as the spouse has not remarried.

9.___F___. The decedent's final income tax return must be filed within six months of his date of death.

10.___T___. The fiduciary of an estate is responsible for the estate tax even if the majority of the estate consists of non-probate property.

11.___F___. The most important consideration in fixing legal fees for estate administration is the time spent on the matter.

12.___T___. A person may only object to an estate accounting if the person will benefit from the objections if they are sustained.

Short Answers

1. If, prior to the issuance of letters testamentary, the named executor realizes that the value of the estate is dropping rapidly because the decedent's investments are depreciating, what should the named executor do, if anything?

> **The named executor should seek preliminary letters to allow him to take action to save the estate assets. Failure to do so could mean that he has breached his fiduciary duty to the estate.**

2. What should an estate executor require before paying a creditor's claim against the estate?

> **The claim must be in writing, must state the facts upon which it is based, and must state the amount claimed. The executor also has the right to request an affidavit proving the claim.**

3. What is ademption? Give an example.

Ademption means that property that is to be disposed of by a will has been disposed of, lost or destroyed prior to death. For example, if the testator's will leaves her diamond ring to her daughter, and the diamond ring has been lost or given to another person prior to the testator's death, the testamentary disposition has adeemed.

4. Which of the following gifts is entitled to income from the date of a decedent's death until distribution? Why or why not?

a. a gift of "$50,000 to my daughter".

No, as it is a general bequest.

b. a gift of "my stock in XYZ Corporation to my sister."

Yes, as it is a specific bequest.

c. a gift of the residuary of an estate.

No, as it is a general bequest.

Chapter 14
Ethical Issues Confronting the Paralegal

Multiple Choice

1. Which of the following jobs cannot be delegated to the paralegal?
a. preparing the first draft of a client's will, using forms prepared by the attorney.
b. conducting the first interview with an estate client, after the attorney has established an attorney-client relationship.
c. appearing on behalf of the client in Surrogate's Court.
d. preparing an draft estate accounting.

2. A statement about a client's wishes concerning her estate made to the attorney in the presence of a paralegal.
a. may be disclosed by the paralegal as she is not an attorney.
b. is not privileged because the paralegal was present.
c. is a privileged communication and should not be disclosed by either the attorney or the paralegal.
d. may be shared by the paralegal with all other employees of the law practice.

3. The attorney-client privilege may be waived
a. by the attorney or the client.
b. only by the client.
c. upon the disability of the client.
d. by any member of the attorney's law practice.

4. The attorney work product
a. may be obtained through disclosure.
b. is a qualified privilege that may be waived by the paralegal.
c. applies only to materials which the attorney keeps locked in his or her office.
d. protects materials that are the unique product of an attorney's learning and professional skills.

5. When a lawyer drafts a will for a client which leaves a gift to the lawyer,
a. the lawyer may proceed with no concerns.
b. the bequest will be void if the lawyer drafts the will.
c. there will be a presumption of undue influence by the lawyer.
d. the lawyer can be disbarred.

6. A lawyer drafting a will for a client
a. may suggest to the client that she serve as executor under the will.
b. creates a presumption of undue influence if she is the executor under the will.
c. must fully disclose to the client the commissions and fees she will receive if she is to serve as executor.
d. may not serve as executor under any circumstances.

116

7. Which of the following would be considered a ministerial action?
a. setting the legal fees in a matter.
b. indexing exhibits for a trial.
c. conducting a deposition.
d. drafting a will.

8. Which of the following would be considered attorney work product?
a. a paralegal's notes of a witness interview.
b. pictures of an accident scene.
c. a description of an accident prepared by the client.
d. the attorney's strategy for trial.

9. If a client wishes to make a substantial bequest to the attorney drafting his will,
a. this is not a problem.
b. the attorney should suggest that the client get independent legal advice and hire another attorney to draft the will.
c. the gift will be void in all circumstances.
d. the gift will be presumed valid.

10. Paralegals
a. are not subject to any ethical standards.
b. are bound by a specific statutory code of conduct in New York.
c. are subject to ethical standards published by several professional organizations.
d. have not been recognized as a separate group of professionals.

True or False.

1.__F__Although a paralegal may not represent a client in court, it is always permissible for a paralegal to appear for a client at an agency hearing.

2.__T__According to the American Bar Association, the practice of law relates to the rendition of services that call for the professional judgment of a lawyer.

3.__F__It is not necessary that a paralegal disclose her status on correspondence to a client.

4.__F__In the absence of an attorney, the paralegal may accept cases for the law practice.

5.__F__If a paralegal prepares the first draft of a will, it is appropriate for him to send this draft to the client if the attorney is too busy to review it.

6.__T__At a trial, it is permissible for a legal assistant to sit at the counsel table and assist the attorney with exhibits and witnesses.

7.__F__The attorney client privilege may be waived by either the attorney or the client.

8.___T___ The attorney client privilege generally terminates at the death of the client.

9.___F___ A report prepared by the client at the attorney's request, describing an accident, constitutes attorney work product.

10.___F___ It is acceptable for a lawyer to accept a case even if she knows that her law partner will likely be a significant witness in the case.

Short Answers

1. Which of the following communications are privileged?

>   a. A letter sent by the client to the attorney and paralegal concerning her ex-husband's abuse in a divorce action? **Yes.**

>   b. A statement about pending litigation made by the client to his attorney and several others at the firm's holiday party? **No.**

>   c. A statement about pending litigation made by the client to his attorney only at the firm's holiday party? **Yes.**

>   d. A private exchange of recipes between the client and her attorney? **No.**

2. Laura is an estates and trust attorney. Her client, for whom she is drafting a will, asks her to serve as executor under his will. Can Laura do this? If so, what precautions should she take?

>   **It is very risky for an attorney drafting a will to serve as fiduciary under the will. The attorney must prove that the appointment was made freely and voluntarily by the client. If there is any suggestion of undue influence, the court may deny the appointment or the payment of commissions. Finally the attorney must disclose to the client that he or she will receive both commissions and legal fees.**

3. What is the difference between attorney work product and material prepared in anticipation of litigation?

>   **Attorney work product consists of materials that are the product of an attorney's learning and professional skills, such as memoranda prepared by the attorney containing his or her opinion, strategy or analysis. Attorney work product is not discoverable.**

>   **Material prepared in anticipation of litigation includes witness statements, notes by witnesses, and notes of witness interviews. These materials are not generally prepared by the attorney and do not involve the attorney's**

professional judgment. They are discoverable upon a showing that the other party needs them to prepare his or her case and has no other access to them.